Pub Walks
in
The Forest of Dean

including East Gwent

Neil Coates

Published by Sigma Leisure – an imprint of
Sigma Press, 1 South Oak Lane, Wilmslow, Cheshire SK9 6AR, England.

British Library Cataloguing in Publication Data
A CIP record for this book is available from the British Library.

ISBN: 1-85058-357-9

Typesetting and Design by: Sigma Press, Wilmslow, Cheshire.

Text photographs: Neil Coates

Cover photograph: The Lion Inn, Trellech (Neil Coates)

Printed & bound by: Manchester Free Press, Longford Trading Estate, Thomas Street, Stretford, Manchester M32 0JT.   Tel: 061-864 4540

General Disclaimer

Whilst every effort has been made to ensure that the information given in this book is correct, neither the publisher nor the author accept any responsibility for any inaccuracy.

PREFACE

I suppose that this book is, really, an indulgence, a celebration of an area of Britain still relatively unknown and undervisited. Next time you're in a large group in your local pub, or wherever, take a straw poll to see who has heard of the Forest of Dean and who can locate it on a map; the result will almost certainly be surprisingly few.

Yet Dean is one of Britain's natural treasures, the greatest tract of native woodland left in these Islands. The verdant treescape fills a wedge of Gloucestershire between the Severn and the Welsh border, its valleys, hills, heaths, pastures and marshlands retaining tantalising glimpses of long gone industries and peoples and hosting most species of mammal, large and small, common and endangered, that there are to be seen. The proximity of the Welsh border, for many centuries a war zone fought over by Kings and courtiers, despots and abbots, ensures a vibrant history and a land amply supplied with castles and abbeys, churches and battlefields.

The walks in this book aim to involve you in exploring and experiencing many of these features, with the considerable added benefit of being based at a convivial hostelry purveying real ale, beer at its best. It's obviously a personal selection of walks and pubs, but one which I hope and trust gives a good overview of much of what the area has to offer.

None of the walks could, by any stretch of the imagination, be classified as strenuous, but most of them include climbs, some of them steep, an unavoidable product of the nature of the local landscape. Your reward may be immense views across South Wales to the highest peaks of the Brecon Beacons, may be tracing the course of the earliest tramroads through sun-dappled glades past tiny freemines, or may be happening upon a riverside pub selling freshly caught and cooked elvers.

Sadly, few of the walks are easily accessible by public transport, those which are have the relevant details at the beginning of the chapter concerned. On schooldays or market days there may be a special service, often a large taxi or minibus, making one return trip. Details of such services in the Gloucestershire area (walks 11-25) may be picked up at Coleford Tourist Information Centre or by telephoning the County Information Line on Gloucester 425543.

Acknowledgements

My own old, trusty boots have carried me over every inch of every walk in this book and across the threshold of each pub (often more than once...). Helping with those arduous tasks of sauntering and imbibing, wayfinding and route checking, visiting pubs and sampling bar meals have been Tim Bassett, Brian Davies, Nicky Smith and Dave Kean, to each of whom many thanks. Thanks also to Jo and Kevin Appleton for endless suggestions for pubs and walks in the Wye Valley area.

My thanks, too, to the proprietors and licensees of the pubs featured in this volume for their hospitality and the gems of local information many of them were eager to pass on; to those few I didn't manage to buttonhole my thanks in absentia!

Much of the background and historical detail in the text comes from living in the area for many years and working on a variety of projects therein, but I must acknowledge the invaluable source and wealth of detail offered by the formidable output of books and papers researched by Dr. Cyril Hart, the Chief Verderer of Dean (especially his "The Industrial History of Dean" [David & Charles, 1971]) and William Dreghorn's "Geology Explained in the Forest of Dean and the Wye Valley" [David & Charles 1968]. H.W.Paar's two books about the area's railways are also a mine of fascinating facts and figures ["The Severn & Wye Railway" (1963), "The Great Western Railway in Dean" (1965), both from David & Charles].

Finally, my grateful thanks to my parents for their encouragement given to me at an early age to go and explore Dean whilst the old industries still clung to life and to learn to appreciate the natural history, geography and geology of the area. To them I dedicate this book.

Neil Coates

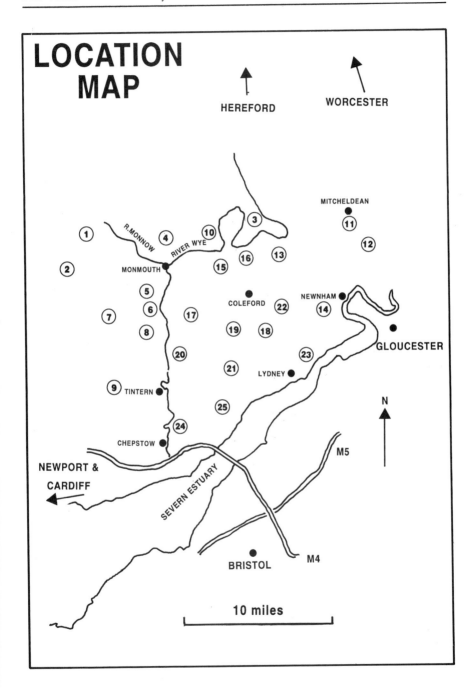

LOCATION MAP

CONTENTS

Background

The Walks

The Forest of Dean and East Gwent

The Walks

The wide variety of landscape, landforms and history of and in Dean and East Gwent is well represented by the walks in this book. None is long enough nor strenuous enough to cause palpitations in those beyond their teenage years, but then neither are they Sunday School rambles, sanitized, cleared of all potential problems and suitable for keeping the patent-leather mirrorlike shine intact on town shoes!

The very nature of the landscape in this area – generally a plateau incised or cut through by countless streams and rivers – means that the majority of the walks inevitably will have muddy sections and some steep and/or lengthy climbs to contend with; particularly challenging ones are highlighted in the titles of each walk. The message is, if you've got walking boots then use them.

All the walks follow public rights of way or, in some cases, take advantage of the right to roam in Forestry Commission areas, in areas included in The Forest of Dean and Wye Valley Forest Park and on common land. Any particular access problems encountered during the researching of the book are highlighted in the text; it is the nature of the animal that is the public footpath, however, that problems arise without notice, as it were.

In general, the Forestry Commission, local authorities, landowners and farmers, the Wye Valley Countryside Service, Parish and Community

Councils, local rambling clubs and volunteers, through their tireless work at waymarking, stile & bridge construction and path clearance, make this area of the Marches a joy to walk in. On the down side, parts of Northeast Gwent are appalling, although recent work around Trellech and Monmouth shows just what can be done given the determination and resources.

The value of long-established public footpaths, bridleways and other rights of way is becoming increasingly recognised by recreational and countryside bodies; the Countryside Commission is currently sponsoring a long term "Parish Paths" project, and one of the target areas is Gloucestershire, so any problems you can highlight to that County Council would be particularly valuable!

If you do come across a problem, on one of these walks or at any other occasion, and you are sure you are on a public right of way, few landowners would object to your making a short detour to circumvent the particular problem encountered (although, strictly, you'd be trespassing). On returning home report the problem to the Rights of Way Officer at the relevant County Council (usually in the Planning, Highways or Surveying Department) to highlight the point at issue.

In the titles to each walk is given the appropriate Ordnance Survey 1:25000 ($2^1/_2$ inches to the mile) Sheet name and/or reference. It's safe to say that the vast majority are to be found on the Outdoor Leisure series Sheet 14, Wye Valley & Forest of Dean. You shouldn't have any problems in completing the walks from the text alone, but the additional information available from a local map always can add to the enjoyment of a ramble.

Pubs, Beers & Breweries

In 1901, there were some 242 pubs and beerhouses in the Forest of Dean. By 1976 this number had shrunk to 143 and currently there are around 130. Their demise was due almost solely to the disappearance of the countless coal and iron mines, forges and furnaces from the Forest. Many of these supported one (or more) beerhouses either on-site or close by, as the works was run down and closed then so too did the drinking arm of the concern disappear; it was not unusual throughout the industrial areas of Britain for the Company to own such recreational facilities, this survives even today in the form of work's clubs open only to employees.

The demise of the Company Beerhouse must have been a boon for the local breweries and their tied estates, but they too, in turn, have succumbed to closures, amalgamations and the vagaries of business practice. The Forest and adjoining areas once hosted dozens of breweries and home-brew establishments, but none now survive.

Perhaps the most commonly found sign on Forest pubs is the multi-coloured, glazed-pottery castle symbol mounted next to the door of many-a-current (and past) pub. This was the trade mark of the West Country Brewery, now a part of the Whitbread empire but which itself had taken over most of the pubs of Dean's major brewer, Wintle's of Mitcheldean. Although this ceased brewing under its own name in the 1920s (the brewery site is now a small part of the huge Rank Xerox plant), its ghost survives – Whitbread's Forest Brown bottled Ale, nationally available, has it's roots in Mitcheldean.

Most other towns, and even villages, had their own local brewhouse or small brewery, Lydney, Chepstow and Ruardean for example. Redbrook had two, an upper and a lower brewery, now evidenced solely by the names of several local houses. In Monmouth's St. Mary's Street an old pub, now a turf accountants, still has a painted facade advertising "Celebrated Redbrook Fine".

Monmouth itself once had several breweries (and, incredibly, around eighty licensed premises) supplying the town and its hinterland. Nearby Ross boasted at least two breweries. All, sadly, are now long gone, the only tangible reminders being an occasional etched pub window, an old brewery mirror or tray over a bar, glass or pottery bottles and flagons on pub shelves or the chance find of medieval beermats in a dusty corner of a local antiques emporium.

The pubs, too, have changed. Few now offer both a lounge and public bar whilst virtually none have escaped the attentions of developers and "improvers" during the last twenty or so years. Notable exceptions to the latter trait include The Cherry Tree in Tintern (near Walk 9), The Ostrich in Newland (on Walk 17) and the New Buildings near Kerne Bridge, south of Ross (near Walk 13 and which retains an Alton Court Brewery sign), all definitely worth searching out.

Whilst Whitbread retains a virtual stranglehold on tied houses in the area, the number of free-houses in and around Dean has increased over recent years. Thus Flowers' IPA, Original and Pale Ale, all brewed at the old Cheltenham and Hereford Brewery in Cheltenham, are widely available in Whitbread houses (a few of wh n also carry Marston's Pedigree) whilst the choice in the free-houses varies considerably. Many offer favourites such as Theakstons, Ruddles or Bass, slightly less common are beers from regional breweries such as Wadworths, Hook Norton, Ushers (recently bought-out by its management from Watneys), Felinfoel and Brains and occasionally offerings from smaller breweries such as Smiles (Bristol), Wye Valley (Hereford), Bull Mastiff (Penarth) and Uley (Dursley).

In this respect the most enterprising freehouse is The Boat Inn, Penallt, on the Welsh side of the Wye over the footbridge from Redbrook, which invariably has a good half-dozen or more different breweries' products on offer.

Car Parking

All but one of the walks in this book start at pubs which have a dedicated car park, ample roadside parking nearby or both. Most licensees are already inured to the fact of walkers leaving their cars in their car parks and disappearing into the wide blue yonder for hours on end. Few object to this practice, but it's only fair, whenever possible, to pop your head around the door and let the landlord or landlady know that this is what you plan to do .... or have a wee tincture before you start out!

The Land of Dean

The Forest of Dean is one of those rare places which has a soul; an immortality born of the timeless wildwood, the threads of which still pervade an area with an aura undiminished by time. Dean is a prescient landscape, one which long ago surrendered up its skin of boundless tracts of oak and its bones of mineral wealth to that transient and ephemeral species, man. Peel away the veneers by which man tries to disguise, to reject, this ancient past, however, and the primal landscape of England is revealed. The soul survives intact beneath the managed greenwood that is today's Dean.

If this all sounds just a bit esoteric then take yourself on a late spring afternoon or a crisp early morning in winter to Forge or Welshbury Woods, Sallowvallets or Highmeadow Inclosures and partake of the experience yourself. The atmosphere can be electric, the silence almost preternatural. Within minutes the rhythm of the Forest asserts itself on the senses, vestiges of a simpler age ooze from your surroundings, the passage of time reverts to being a trivial matter of little significance. The geological plateau that hosts Dean seems to exist almost on another plane.

Bounding Dean to the west is the River Wye, trapped in its tortuous, wooded gorge as it flows towards the sea, carrying with it vestiges of the high Cambrian Mountains of Wales, reduced to silt and mud by the ravages of time and weather. Here, if anywhere in the region, the ancient wildwood survives; not even the supremely inventive charcoal burners and miners of old could contrive to strip the precipitous slopes of this famous gorge of the native forest. Centuries old yew trees cling to the slopes or grow at remarkable angles from the faces of limestone crags; contorted, wraith-like oaks, bearded with mosses and lichen contrive to hold the very earth together with their twisted, gnarled roots whilst hangars of massive beech hold up the sky.

A step westwards again and Dean's dissected plateau comes to an abrupt end, as if great scoops had been taken from the edge of the world which is this Forest's boundary. These great, steep embayments, scarps of sandstone and conglomerate, sweep down to the Vale of Gwent, a verdant mosaic of fields and woodlands, tiny villages dominated by the

An old, walled trackway above the River Wye

gaunt remains of Norman castles and market towns dating back nearly two millenia. Here and there isolated hills, outliers of sandstone, loom large over this landscape whilst the horizon rears up as the massive wall that is the Black Mountains and, beyond, the Brecon Beacons, far into South Wales. The Vale is drained largely by the River Trothy (Troddi) which meanders its way eastwards to join the Wye near Monmouth, further south the Olway and its tributaries trend southwestwards to issue into the Usk near Usk.

To the east and south Dean bows to the jurisdiction of the mighty River Severn. The great sandbanks and mudflats, one of Europe's most important wildfowl sanctuaries (the world-famous Slimbridge Wildfowl Trust is on the eastern bank of the estuary opposite Blakeney) are washed by the second highest tides in the world (surpassed only by the tidal range in the Bay of Fundy, Canada). Here, Dean's fortress like plateau looks out over a narrow strip of lowland between wood and river, a rolling landscape of venerable old farms and small estuarine ports which developed purely to ease the passage of Dean's mineral wealth of centuries past to the industrial complexes of the West Country and South Wales. It's a little visited, almost forgotten land, an area threaded by narrow, high-hedged by-ways and crisscrossed by age old tracks and pathways leading to and through gentle valleys and winding creeks (pills) which feather the shoreline of the estuary.

This leaves the northern extremity of the Forest to be delineated. Here, no obvious physical boundary can be said to mark the edge of the realm of Dean. Instead, the plateau gradually surrenders to the lower lands of south Herefordshire and Gloucestershire as a fragmented landscape, a great arc of wooded hills interspersed by a complex network of streams which eventually drain westwards to the Wye or eastwards to the River Leadon and thence the Severn. Here the hills of May, Penyard and Breakheart shelter scattered communities with such delightful names as Dancing Green and Yartleton, Hope Mansell and Aston Crews, many of which have histories dating back to the Normans and boast houses nearly as old. This northern part also hosts the highest point in the Forest, Ruardean Hill at 951 feet, in itself no famous viewpoint nor obvious feature but simply one of the knuckles of slightly higher land which mark the northern end of the contiguous woodlands of Dean.

Such, then, is Dean. A plateau of modest elevation isolated from such renowned uplands as the Cotswolds, the Malvern Hills and the Black Mountains by tracts of lowland resulting from the times of the glaciers; The Vale of Gwent and the Herefordshire Plain owe much of their fertility to boulder clay deposited by ice-sheets only about 15000 years ago. The Severn Estuary has only existed, as such, since then; before that time the Severn flowed northwards into what is now Liverpool Bay, copious glacial meltwater overflowing southwards forged its current course between Dean and the Cotswolds.

In winter snowstorms can cut the area off for days on end; spring sees this white mantle replaced by the myriad colours of a forest ecosystem at its best. Swathes of wild daffodil and snowdrop, bluebell and ramson, primrose and anemone carpet the floor of the woodland that is one of England's two great broadleaf forests, an area dappled in summer with rich haymeadows and bounded by estuarine wetlands and crack-willow lined streams. Autumn sees summer's ever-greener tresses of myriad leaves slowly replaced by one of nature's great spectacles, that arboreal final fling of reds and ochres, yellows and golds before the trees batten down once more against the ravages of winter.

Visitors to this natural wonderland are nothing new. Many know of Wordsworth's poem "Lines composed a few miles above Tintern Abbey..."; he was but a latecomer on the Wye Tour, an outing first organised by a vicar of Ross-on-Wye in the early 1700s for the benefit of the gentility who would make the sometimes arduous overland journey from Bristol or Gloucester to Ross-on-Wye. Here they would join a skiff or small boat for a two or three day voyage downriver via Monmouth to Chepstow, stopping, perhaps, at Goodrich Castle and Flanesford Priory, Monmouth, Llandogo and Tintern. One such voyager was William Gilpin, the celebrated Eighteenth Century travelling curate whose writings and diaries had a profound effect on the likes of Wordsworth and Ruskin a century and more later.

Few writers or visitors of this era diverged from this standard tour to explore the Forest of Dean; transport was unsure, thick woodland/forest less of a novelty than it is today and, besides, industry was ravaging the plateau, a fact acknowledged by Gilpin, for example, who commented on the size of Wyeside forges/furnaces near Symonds Yat. In Ruskin's time (c. 1880) the Wye Valley Railway all but killed off water borne tourist and commercial traffic on the river, but largely failed to capitalise on the romance or reputation of the Valley to "milk" an increasingly mobile public. The writings of Fletcher Moss, the renowned Manchester antiquarian, traveller and cleric of the early 1900s reflect this, his copious observations on these southern Marches are well worth seeking out.

The motor car, in turn, killed off the railway and fuelled the mass tourism of today and the (re)discovery of Dean. In keeping with the area's rather select history, however, the Forest and the Lower Wye Valley are "also-rans" in terms of visitor numbers and pressures. It may not seem this way on a Bank Holiday or a fine summer Sunday when Tintern and Symond's Yat are heaving and the region's roads "chocka," but on most days of the year it's easy to melt away from the crowds to find the peace and solitude which make this area one of southern Britain's great natural resources. This book is aimed at helping you to do so.

Flora & Fauna

One creature you're bound to see a lot of in Dean is sheep, largely Welsh Mountain, Speckled Faced or Cheviots but occasionally Kerrys or Ryeland. This latter breed are fairly localised, in Britain, to these southern Marches; on their backs was founded great monastic wealth in medieval times, their wool was prized far and away above the fleece of any other breed in the "List of Pegaloti," a sort of fifteenth century EEC standard for medieval Europe's premier industry. Today sheep, and pigs, enjoy the privilege of virtually free-ranging in the Forest to forage for fallen acorn, hazel, beechmast and other ovine/porcine delicacies. An ancient Right of Pannage offers commoners of the Forest the right to graze their own stock on such fruits of the forest; one estimate gives a population of 10000 sheep and 250 pigs. In theory at least they also have precedence on roads, so if you run down a sheep or pig you should make all good efforts to find the owner! You're as likely to come across sheep and lambs resting on the roadside in a town/village centre as you are in Forest pastures and glades.

Such domesticated creatures are, of course, only the tip of that proverbial iceberg when considering the great variety of fauna in Dean. Think of forest animals and most people think of deer. In and around Dean may be found most kinds of deer England can offer. Fallow abound, particularly in the north and west of the Forest; autumn – the rutting season – is the time they are least worried by man and the easiest time to see them, but patience (and a little luck) should reward you at most times of year, especially early morning or evening. There are said to be a few red deer, probably descended from stock which escaped from a large estate, some timid roe deer and a good number of muntjac (Chinese Water Deer), a tiny deer originating in the orient.

Rarely seen but relatively common are badgers, you're more likely to see one as the vergeside victim of a road incident rather than one scuttling through the undergrowth. The remaining oak and beech woodland hosts many setts, most easily identified by the often considerable spoil heaps near the entrances, badgers being scrupulously clean animals. Your best chance to see badgers is probably as a member of a small, organised watch, details of which are held at the various Information Centres in the area.

The usual crop of smaller animals shelter in the trees and pastures; grey and red squirrels, voles, hedgehogs, foxes and suchlike are common. If you know what you're looking for there are also dormice, mink and even polecats. One other kind of mammal rarely given a second thought are bats. Several species make a home in Dean, living in caves and old mine workings, hollow trees and old railway tunnels. They're most easily seen hunting at dusk over many of the ponds, lakes, streams and rivers in the area. All three British snakes live in the Forest, as do several kinds of lizard. Choose a hot, still summer's afternoon and visit one of the myriad small old quarries for a good chance of finding these reptiles, particularly slow-worms, basking in the sunlight.

The Wye and Severn are renowned for various types of aquatic life. The Wye is often cited as one of the top salmon rivers in Britain, certainly the amount paid for fishing rights reflects this reputation. Putchers, sets of funnel-like wicker baskets mounted on frames in the inter-tidal range (i.e. between low & high tide levels) are still set in a few places to catch salmon by a handful of licensed operators on the Severn between Chepstow and Newnham; there was once a thriving Putt-making works at nearby Westbury.

Both rivers come alive with elvers (baby eels) in early summer; in recent years the run of such has decreased but you will still see people in late evening hanging lanterns and torches from the river banks, by doing so attracting the tiny fish to their capacious hand-held nets. A few pubs still occasionally offer elvers fried in butter as a delicacy.

Rare Allis and Thwaite Shad also enter these two river systems in the spring, only a small handful of other rivers in Britain ever see these fish, distantly related to herring. There are a few otter holts on the Wye and its tributaries but these delightful animals are rarely seen, usually evidence comes solely from pawprints, fish remains, spoor and suchlike. The otter's diet was it's downfall; until the late 1960s at least there was a pack of otter hounds active along the Monnow Valley, supported by river keepers and riparian owners determined to boost stocks of game fish at the ultimate cost to otters.

Bird life obviously makes the most of the varied potential of Dean's wooded plateau and its attendant cliffs, valleys, meadows and estuaries. At Nagshead, near Parkend, is a major RSPB reserve based in mature oak woodland, whilst in Great Kensley Enclosure, near Speech House in the very centre of the Forest, is Woorgreens Lake, the flooded remains of opencast coal workings worked until the 1970s but now an important location for wildfowl.

These semi-organised locations are obviously the best place to go to guarantee seeing a variety of species. If you know what you're about, however, and/or have a bit of good fortune, then you may see any of a hundred and more species in the area of Dean, from larger species such as buzzard, heron and various swans to tiny nuthatches, goldcrest, treecreepers and wrens. Essentially more noisy varieties are also commonly seen (or, at least, heard); jays, the rapid knocking of the greater and lesser spotted woodpeckers or the raucous laugh of the green woodpecker, the screeching of barn and little owls and that all-time favourite, the hoot of the tawny owl.

More rarely, the unique call of the nightjar (oft described as akin to a small motorbike engine being revved over and over again) may be heard on a summer's evening (Trellech Beacon, west of the Wye, was a good spot in the summer of 1992). Symond's Yat is one of those rare places where Peregrine Falcons nest; if you're very lucky you may catch one "stooping," in other words diving from the sky towards unwary prey (which they always take on the wing). You'll need a quick eye, however, as it's Britain's fastest bird, stooping at an estimated 180 mph.

Afficianadoes of waterfowl find the Severn Estuary a paradise, particularly in winter when it is one of Europe's most important overwintering sites, one reason why the famous Slimbridge Wildfowl Trust is now long-established on the opposite side of the estuary to Dean. The Forest side has its fair share, however, of many species of waders, Canada and white-fronted geese and numerous types of duck.

Woodland

Few of Dean's trees are of any great age. The odd stand of venerable old yews and the occasional twisted, gnarled oak may date back to before the Civil War but in general today's Forest is a manicured landscape rather than a remnant of medieval forest or wildwood.

A Forestry Road

This is not to say that the woodland lacks character, interest or history. Far from it, in fact; many of the steeper, more inaccessible woods that clothe the Wye Gorge are amongst the oldest surviving broadleaf woodlands in Britain, only marginally affected by man's activities during the past millenium.

The great importance ascribed to the Forest's timbers by naval boatbuilders since Henry II established the Senior Service ensures a long history of care, management and development of the timber resource, today (at the time of writing, at least) undertaken largely by the Forestry Commission who took over from the grandiosely-titled "Commissioners of Woods, Forests and Land Revenues of the Crown" in 1919.

From the Sixteenth Century onwards, several Acts of Parliament have been passed dealing specifically with the Forest of Dean, aimed at controlling coppicing, protecting stocks of mature oak, managing the output of iron, policing the grazing of livestock and numerous other related issues. Ancient laws, some based on the Forest Law of Saxon and Norman times, were revived and renewed, often overseen and implemented by the Verderers Court which still meets at Speech House, now a hotel but originally built in 1676 specifically to house the meetings and Courts of these Forest managers, overseers and justices.

Thus at various times all forges and furnaces were destroyed, or the commoners rights of pannage suspended from vast areas of woodland "inclosed" for timber management purposes (hence the many named "Inclosures" in today's Forest). The Verderers (of which there are four) look after the "Vert" of the Forest (the trees and the deer) whilst the Gavellers (two) control the extractive industries.

Most of today's broadleaf woodland dates from early Victorian days, when wooden-hulled ships still ruled the waves and Brunel's (amongst others) faith in and experimentation with iron ships was in its infancy. Nelson visited the Forest in 1802 and was appalled by the state of the timber reserves in this vital storehouse for the navy's future vessels. Largely as a result of his criticisms huge planting schemes were initiated. Successive management regimes have produced the country's most outstanding tract of forest, one still being worked very hard as a valuable natural resource.

Outside the "core" areas of mature beech and oak are great tracts of conifers, fast-growing species resulting in dark, rather gloomy places often disguised behind veneers of the older broadleaf woodland. Dean has few naturally-occurring native conifers, simply because over thousands of years the dominant climatic regime favoured the success of broadleaf species. The few stands of old, mature firs which do exist are largely a product of planting in the 1700s.

In keeping with Dean's primacy it was declared a National Forest Park in 1938, the first designation of such a Park in Britain. As the Forestry Commission currently owns much of the woodland there is virtually unrestricted access to much of the area, leaving the visitor free to wander at will in England's great forest. The Commission's stewardship ensures that recreational provision is managed in a manner in keeping with the resource; visitor facilities are concentrated at a few key sites leaving much of the woodland in as semi-natural a state as possible.

Perhaps half of the Forest's total area (about 35000 acres) is broadleaf woodland, vast tracts of oak and beech, sycamore and limes, hornbeam and wych elm cloaking deep, winding valleys and ridges and reclaiming old tramroads, railways and industrial sites. Away from the forestry roadways and tracks it's very easy to imagine that you've discovered a surviving stand of Britain's medieval woodland. Whilst the majority of coniferous plantations are characterless there are stands of, for example, Douglas Fir and Scots Pine which positively enhance the Forest, some of these date back more than two centuries. It's relevant, too, not to overlook the fact that the thick, gloomy conifers do play their part in offering the Forest's deer a valuable refuge and place to hide in relative safety. Reflecting the great variety of trees in Dean, the arboretum at Speech House displays over 200 species.

To get the most out of Dean's woodlands you have to be prepared to follow your nose. "Armchair ramblers" can simply park up at a roadside pull-in or picnic area and vestiges of the forest will come to them; the hemming-in trees will deliver animal and bird life and myriad shades of leaves to your dashboard picnic table. Making the effort to walk along the well maintained forestry roads brings a new dimension, with the swathes of woodspurge and dog's mercury, foxglove and hellebore, or the chance of seeing countless birds or stumbling across abandoned industrial sites and road-cuttings exposing bands of coal or ochre.

The most dedicated, however, simply follow indistinct tracks and paths deep into the forest. They are the most amply rewarded, with the chance of seeing the larger mammals, happening upon great carpets of bluebell and ramson, of finding hidden ponds and bogs rich in damp-loving plants, dragonflies and reptiles, or of stumbling into peaceful, little visited sun-dappled glades shaded by giant beech and oak trees.

The choice is yours.

A Geological Overview

Trying to cut corners and give a generalised overview of the geology of any area is a practice both fraught with difficulties and pockmarked with pitfalls. Of few areas is this more true than the Forest of Dean and Lower Wye Valley. Whilst the overall structure is, in geological terms, fairly simple, any number of localised variations combine to make the area one favoured by those in the business of teaching geology as a place to train field geologists, to study classic structures and to practice and perfect mapping skills. It's a fair bet that if you spend any time in the area you'll encounter school parties seeking ammonites and plant fossils or lone undergraduates toiling to discern the underlying structure and localised rock types.

Essentially the area is a great syncline, or bowl, of sandstone rock dating from the Devonian period of the geological "clock," about 370 million years ago when the area was part of a great desert. The edges of this bowl act as the edge of the raised plateau which is Dean, a fortress of more resistant rock standing out from the younger, weaker strata more quickly eroded away and thus lowered by the ravages of climate and time. Lining this bowl is a thick layer of limestone, deposited during the Carboniferous period about 320 million years ago. By this time the desert regime had been replaced by a shallow tropical sea rich in microscopic lifeforms which helped produce the limestone. This horseshoe-shaped limestone structure hosts the deposits of iron ore and ochre for which the Forest was renowned.

The middle of the bowl, and the central area of the Forest of Dean, is infilled by what are referred to as the Coal Measures. As the name suggests these rocks host the coal seams once so important to the economic life of the plateau, but the name conceals a complicated mix of sandstones and limestones, shales and conglomerates dating from the Upper Carboniferous and Triassic eras on the geological clock, around 220-280 million years ago.

At this time the area was a part of a massive system of swamps and deltas at the edge of a great landmass. The swamps and deltas existed in the sort of hot, humid conditions found today in tropical rainforests, the profuse vegetation dying, rotting down and being compressed into shales and coal very quickly, this process being repeated time and again over millions of years.

The landmass was unstable and subject to swift erosion by immense rivers which deposited great swathes of sand and silt over the fetid swamplands, in turn being recovered by further tropical forests and swamps. Thus a great layered cake was built up, of coals and shales, sandstones and conglomerates, to fill the heart of the great sandstone syncline. The resultant coal seams varied in thickness from a few inches to the four-foot plus thickness of the High Delf seam, the Forest's most productive source.

Geology being geology the full story is, of course, not nearly so simple or cut and dried. Within the Dean area are countless faults which all but render the above geological sketch irrelevant. The movement of landmasses over relatively recent geological time (around 280 million years ago) ensure that the great syncline plays host to smaller anticlines (upfolds) and periclines, unconformities and, in the case of May Hill, a remnant of far older rocks of the Silurian era.

The shape of the landscape is largely governed by the underlying geology and the structures therein. Thus many of the deep, narrow valleys which dissect Dean's plateau follow the lines of faults and/or bands of weaker, more erodible rock, cleaving down through aeons of time and often exposing the narrow coal seams and bands of different rock types in the valley sides; some of these coal seams thus exposed form the basis of free mines here and there in the depths of the Forest.

The most famous feature of the whole area is the Wye Gorge, a great wound in the surface of the plateau coursing for about twenty five miles before abruptly issuing into the Severn estuary near Chepstow. About three million years ago the gorge didn't exist. At that time sea level was considerably higher than it is now and the proto-Wye meandered sluggishly across a great plain. Climatic changes on a worldwide scale resulted in a gradual fall in overall sea level, estimated at some 600 feet to the present day.

As the sea level fell the river became increasingly erosive. At the same time, however, it largely retained its historical course, flowing over the sandstones, brownstones and conglomerates around (present day)

Hereford and Ross and the mixture of older, more resistant limestones and sandstones of today's Forest. The result was that the river eroded the softer rocks away more completely and thoroughly than the harder ones, thus creating the undulating plain of Herefordshire to the north of Dean and cutting down through the lime and sandstones like a cheese wire, creating the Wye gorge to the south. The renowned viewpoint of Yat Rock offers an excellent prospect over both these features.

As the sea level continued to fall so did the efficacy of this action increase. The main gorge reflects the original course of the "old" Wye, superimposed or incised into the plateau. Here and there this action was so efficient and concentrated that large meanders (loops) of the river were cut off at the neck, the narrowest point of the loop. The main river continued to cut downwards into the plateau and left these old loops high and dry, known as "abandoned meanders". The best example is that in which now lies the village of Newland, southeast of Monmouth. These abandoned loops of the Wye now host smaller, less erosive streams which course their way down to the main river over long stretches of shoots and falls, such as those at Cleddon which sweep down from the heights of Trellech's plateau.

The contrast between these gorges, incised valleys and folded landscapes and the undulating Vale of Gwent, to the west of Trellech is stark. Here, thick beds of Old Red Sandstone (about 380 million years old) have lain all-but undisturbed by geological folding, faulting or sculpting, leaving a gentle land of pleasing convexities enriched but unaltered by the ice-sheets of old, a geological pause for breath, as it were, between the complexities of Dean and the mountains of South Wales.

And if the Wye is young then the Severn, at least in its present form, is a veritable infant. Only at the end of the last great ice age, just 15,000 years ago, did the great river we know today come into being. A vast periglacial lake of meltwater formed in the area around present-day Shrewsbury and Telford in amounts much too great to drain off northwards towards Liverpool along the then-existing river course which was, in any case, all but blocked by the retreating ice-sheet. Another way out was needed, and the waters breached the line of low-lying hills around Bridgnorth, creating the famous Ironbridge Gorge, following (and greatly widening) the courses of various smaller rivers and, finally, usurping the lower course of the old River Avon to create today's Severn Estuary, Dean's eastern boundary.

Man in the Landscape

Man has been around in the area of Dean for a very long time. Here and there may be found the ubiquitous standing stones, de rigeur in any claim to long history and great antiquity. The Queen Stone near Goodrich, The Long Stone near Staunton, the Broad Stone at Wibdon and Harold's Stones at Trellech for example all are dated back to the Bronze Age.

As ever, their function is totally unknown; Harold's Stones are recognised by some authorities as the remains of a long-barrow; folklore insists they are three wrongdoers turned to stone by a white witch, or even stones hurled in fury by the legendary Jack o' Kent from the summit of the Skirrid Mountain near Abergavenny. The Long Stone is said to bleed if pricked at midnight by a needle; superstition, perhaps, based on dark practices and blood sacrifices made at the stone thousands of years ago.

Predating these edifices is a small cave cut by the River Wye into the limestone of The Doward, near Whitchurch, hundreds of thousands of years ago. Known as King Arthur's Cave it has been used as a shelter by both man and beast for at least sixty thousand years, evidenced by the remains of such as cave bear, lion and giant hyena, palaeolithic hand axes and arrow heads (Monmouth Museum has many such relics). These stone age peoples were the first known inhabitants of Dean.

The hill they lived on also hosts the remains of a much more recent construction, a hill fort dating back a mere 2500 years or so. This is one of a series of such settlements around the periphery of the Forest, others can be found at Lancaut, Yat Rock and Welshbury Wood. The name of this latter one is interesting; bury is Old English for settlement, the prefix Welsh suggests an origin as a base for families of welsh speakers still living in the area at a time when such facts became significant.

These native Celts shared the countryside with the Romans, whose presence in Dean was almost entirely due to the wealth of iron ore known to exist in the area. They developed essentially small scale, but still significant, opencast workings between Bream and Lydney and at other sites scattered around the Forest where the Crease Limestone or Lower Dolomite rock outcrops.

Doubtless some of this ore was transported to other parts of the Empire on ships via the Wye and Severn; there is evidence that much smelting took place at the Roman settlement at Ariconium, just north of present-day Weston under Penyard. The course of a Roman Road has been recognised running from here through the Forest to the Severn at Lydney; what is often claimed to be a section of this road is exposed at Blackpool Bridge, two miles east of Parkend.

Other roads are assumed to have linked the major Roman settlements at Gloucester, Caerleon and Caerwent (near Chepstow). In the immediate area of Dean, Temples have been found at Littledean, Huntsham and Lydney Park, whilst Monmouth was the site of the trading and military centre of Blestium.

The Celts outlasted the Romans in the west of Dean by several centuries, the area immediately west of the Wye is littered with place name evidence; prefixes such as Llan (Llangrove), Tre (Tretire) and Pen (Penallt) abound and all are of Welsh origin. The Saxon King, Offa, was more than a little worried by the Welsh. Borrowing an idea from his father, who had built a series of ditches across the neck of Denmark to keep the uncivilised rabble out of his Germanic domain, Offa junior had constructed his renowned Dyke between the Dee estuary in the north and the Severn estuary in the south.

Nominally, its purpose was to delineate the border between Saxon Mercia and Celtic Wales; in practice it may have had more of an economic function by which tolls and taxes could be levied on the abundant cross-border trade. The sites of many (toll) gates have been recognised by archaeologists working on this, Britain's longest ancient monument.

The most spectacular remaining sections of the Dyke are to be found in mid Wales; good sections are also to be found, however, along the top of the thickly-wooded steep slopes and cliffs east of the Wye between Brockweir and Chepstow. In some places the river itself acted as the barrier.

To these Saxons we owe the original concept of today's Forest. It was they who first set aside great tracts of (largely forested) countryside as hunting preserves for the king and his favourites, areas where commoners could still live and work but killed forest livestock or felled too many trees at pain of death. The Normans continued and codified this legacy, applying their notorious "Forest Law" in addition to the common law of the land. Thus "Forest" applied not just to areas of woodland but to any area, even heath and moorland, subject to this law. In Dean, as in other areas, trees by no means covered all the territory of the Forest, and this remains true to this day.

As ever, it was the Normans and their successors who had the most profound effect on pre-industrial Dean. Even before the Norman Conquest in 1066, that essentially alien feature, the castle, had made an appearance in Britain; the earthen mound (motte) and ramparts (bailey) at Ewyas Harold, about twelve miles west of Ross-on-Wye and dating from around 1050, is one of the claimants to the title of first castle in the country.

The area in and around Dean is exceptionally rich in reminders of these troubled times. Chepstow Castle is one of the greatest of the Marcher Castles. The Marches were essentially self-governing states within Norman England, overlorded by three great Marcher Lords based at these castles. The FitzOsbern family held sway at Chepstow and ensured the "Normanization" of the area.

Any number of the earth and wood motte and bailey castles appeared in the area during the ensuing two centuries – at Trellech, Littledean and English Bicknor for example – whilst sturdier, stone castles were built at many sites, St Briavels, Monmouth, Goodrich and Wilton are all extant examples.

The Normans also consolidated and extended the monastic system which, in the medium term, took over many of the functions of the Marcher Lords and border barons. The Dean area bristled with Abbeys, Priories and Granges, the monks and friars of which were skilled agriculturalists and early industrialists.

The most famous Abbey is, of course, Tintern, that vast Cistercian House nestling in the Wye gorge. At the other end of the Forest was Flaxley Abbey, near Littledean. Flanesford Priory and Monmouth Priory are other existing reminders of this religious dominance, others survive only in place names such as Trellech Grange and Grace Dieu Park. These religious houses made their fortunes from wool, farming sheep in great parklands cleared from the forested areas of the Dean plateau and adjoining areas. Today's pastoral scenery to the east of the Wye between Coleford and Chepstow, for example, was created from the forest at the behest of the monks at Tintern whose flocks of Ryeland sheep created great wealth. This is reflected in the great church at Newland, out of all proportion to the tiny village it serves but built on such a vast scale in celebration of such ovine bounty.

Neither were these monks blind to the riches afforded by industrial development. Laying claim to being the country's, if not the world's, first wireworks is a site in the Angiddy Valley, a sharp defile cut into the plateau to the west of Tintern. The site was developed by the Cistercian Brothers of the nearby Abbey perhaps as early as the Thirteenth Century; a limited amount of ore was won locally, the balance brought in from the other side of the Wye. The series of old ponds, leats and furnaces now partially excavated date from a much later period.

The monks of Flaxley also indulged in the mining and smelting of ore at a site redeveloped centuries later by the Foley family, renowned ironmasters and leading players in the development of the British iron and steel industry before and during the Industrial Revolution.

A short account of Dean's history from this Revolution onwards is given elsewhere in this book. Contemporary Deanman views the timber resource of the Forest in much the same way as his forebearers, as an invaluable asset to be carefully managed and utilised accordingly. Other Forest industries and undertakings have, however, progressed with the times. Employment is now largely in "environment-friendly" manufacturing and service industries. One quirk is the importance of the cardboard-manufacturing industry locally .... largely using paper imported from Canada and Finland. Forest-produced timber commonly goes to newsprint, pine furniture and as the bulk of the veneer or laminate-covered boards beloved of DIY enthusiasts.

Whilst myriad small industrial estates foster an employment base for the area, Dean is increasingly a land of absentee-workers, wealthy commuters who benefit from the swift motorway access to Birmingham, Bristol and Cardiff, all now less than an hour's drive from the centre of the Forest. Much of Dean's early history was one of exclusivity, a playground for royalty and the rich who enjoyed their patronage. Things seem to have come almost full circle; the desirability of and quality of life available in Dean today means few miners or foresters (for example) could now afford to move into the area, nor Dean-born folk afford to stay. Such a fact lies uneasily with the insular outlook that Forest folk cultivate; you've got to be Forest born and bred to be considered a true man of Dean.

Increasingly, the Forest's exclusivity grows year on year. The danger is that the disintegration of the Forestry Commission's landholdings will compound this trend until a day arrives when trees will become a barrier against, and not offer a silent welcome to, the majority of people. Whither then the rights of pannage or the time-out-of-mind traditions of the Freeminers; whither then the accepted freedom to roam in publicly-owned woodland and common land? The Ordnance Survey no longer identifies Forestry Commission woodlands on its new and revised maps, as if conflict were already imminent. What price then a walk along a Dean path or the Speech House Sculpture trail in years to come?

Enjoy Dean, its character, friendliness and welcome before that unpalatable day finally dawns.

Scratching the Industrial Surface

The Forest today is in probably the most peaceful and quiet state it has known since early medieval times. A century ago men beavered away in underground levels, delved great holes in the earth and piled high spoil and waste in miniature ranges of mountains beneath and around the trees, whilst furnaces, forges and chemical works belched forth into an atmosphere heady with noxious fumes.

Almost every valley hosted horse drawn tramroads or steam engines scurrying along twisting trackways, carrying the produce of the Forest to thriving little ports and wharves for export throughout the Empire and beyond. Even thirty years ago major pits still survived and tank engines toiled up the steep gradients from the Severn to the depths of the Forest.

All is now gone. Dean is one of Britain's lost industrial landscapes. The area didn't suffer the savagery that characterises contemporary changes imposed on an area's industry by outmoded, detached, doctrinaire political whim. Rather, a relatively gentle, almost natural decline occurred, no less harsh on the people and communities affected but a harshness tempered by alternatives and an acceptance of the dynamics of change on a timescale to which those affected could relate.

Reflecting this, Dean's population has remained virtually static from the heyday of its industrial epoch at the turn of this Century to the present day, around 43000 people. The social make-up of this population will obviously have changed considerably this century, but this continuity of population size is rare in an old rural industrial area, contrasting sharply with the experiences of other similar areas such as Cornwall, the North Pennines and Cumberland for example, where the decline of traditional industries led to serious depopulation.

Dean's industries were largely based on the area's natural resources of timber and minerals. A plethora of enterprises both large and small, common-a-day and out-of-the-ordinary have seen Dean's importance rise and fall, waver and stabilise over at least the past two thousand years. There is space here for only the briefest of outlines.

The Romans knew of the Forest's iron ore and coal, possibly from records available to them of trade undertaken by earlier traders such as the Phoenicians. Certainly one of the primary reasons for the Roman presence in Britain was the availability of minerals such as iron ore, and Dean became an important source.

Shallow workings worked by (or for) these Latins survive at various places around the horseshoe-shaped outcrop of ore-bearing rock stamped on Dean, areas known as scowles. The best examples are around Bream (where a hoard of Roman coins was discovered in 1854) and in the great estate of Lydney Park, other sites exist in the Wigpool area north of Mitcheldean.

Whilst these sites haven't exactly been mothballed since 400 A.D., medieval miners simply extended the Roman workings or developed new ones of their own on the Crease Limestone deposits.

The importance of the iron industry increased substantially from late medieval times onwards, when the first deep mines were sunk. Certainly by the time of Good Queen Bess (Elizabeth I) so much charcoal was being produced to enable the ore to be smelted that severe restrictions were imposed on both mining and burning in order to protect the supply of timber.

This was not so much with an eye to the future well-being of the miners and charcoal burners, as to safeguarding the supply of timbers for the Navy, the Forest of Dean being a prime source for such a purpose (it is said that the destruction of Dean's oaks was a high priority both of the Spanish Armada in 1588 and of Napoleon's army of invasion in the early 1800s).

Matching the Forest's coal (in the form of coke) with its iron ore took place relatively late in comparison to other areas; it was nearly a century after Abraham Darby's great experiments at Coalbrookdale and Iron-bridge in the early 1700s that coke fired furnaces became established in Dean, largely due to the relatively poor coking quality of the locally mined coal.

The consequent great improvement in the amount of iron extractable from the ore (due to the higher temperatures attainable from smelting with coke rather than charcoal) led to the rapid development of both the coal and iron mining industries. Iron's zenith was reached in the 1870s when upwards of 200,000 tons was produced annually; coal peaked around the turn of the century with over one million tons raised each year.

Decline set in mainly due to failing resources as much as competition from the gigantic developments in the valleys of South Wales, where massive mining and smelting industries were complemented with large scale iron and steel works and ease of export of the products only dreamt of by the workers of Dean's industry. It's more than coincidence, however, that the great ironmasters of South Wales, the Crawshays and the Foleys, cut their teeth in Dean's coal and iron industries.

The last iron furnace was raked out in about 1900 although mining continued sporadically, for example at Clearwell, until the end of the Second War. The coal mines fared slightly better, the last major pit closing on Christmas Day 1965, a depressing gift for the 700 or so employees of Northern United Colliery near Cinderford. Now only those anachronistic freeminers remain as the sole inheritors of this proud industrial history. These, and the gritty, workaday towns such as Cinderford, Lydbrook and Ruspidge which fill valley floors and cling to hillsides as if transplanted from the Welsh mining valleys.

Industrial Archaeology

There are too, of course, the poignant remains of this Dean of yesteryear to remind of past glories. The Forest is dotted with the old spoil tips of the coal and iron mines. The vast majority of them are surprisingly difficult to spot, being well landscaped and/or smothered by conifer plantations which are one of the few things to grow in the tips, at Cannop and Mirystock for example.

These "coal alps" at the former New Fancy Colliery, east of Parkend, have even been developed by the Forestry Commission as a viewpoint offering splendid views over much of the Forest. Wherever you wander in Dean you'll almost certainly find evidence, large or small, of coal and iron industry; a fallen building here, a boggy depression there and, in a few places, large areas yet awaiting efforts at reclamation.

Many of the Forest's lakes and ponds were first created to act as header reservoirs. The picturesque scenes at Soudley Ponds, south of Cinderford, and Cannop Ponds, east of Coleford would be less-so without the sheets of water there. All were created to supply water to turn giant waterwheels which, in turn, provided the blast for the Forest's great iron furnaces. The large reedy lake at Woorgreens, near Speech House, results from the recent flooding of opencast coal workings, it's now a nature reserve.

Here and there are perhaps more tangible ghosts of the past. At Clearwell the Old Ham Iron Mine, one of the last to produce ore commercially, is now popular with visitors who can don helmet and overalls and visit the old underground caverns. At nearby Whitecliff are the remains of one of the earliest of the coke furnaces in Dean, where much of Clearwell's ore may have been smelted. The woodlands around Bream hide large areas of the old medieval, even Roman, ironworkings christened scowles (see above) whilst Parkend retains an imposing building associated with the old furnaces there.

The most tangible remains, however, must be the web of old railways and tramroads built to serve the extractive industries. The line between Parkend and Lydney remained in use as a mineral line by B.R. until the 1970s, it is now the base of the Dean Forest Railway whose collection of locos, carriages and wagons are housed at Norchard (at the site of an old colliery and electricity works) and steamed regularly during the year. Apart from this and a short section of the old Wye Valley Railway from Chepstow to quarries near Tidenham, all that remains of the hundreds of miles of track is the main line along the west bank of the Severn. Most of the rest closed in the '50s and '60s, but you can still follow many of the trackbeds deep into the Forest, or stumble unexpectedly over old bridges, tunnels and wharves heavily disguised under decades of ivy and saplings.

In places, evocative remains of horse drawn tramroads survive. The stone block-sleepers still in situ in Bixlade (Bicslade) Valley, near Parkend, carried their iron rails until 1946. The solid old incline at Redbrook is a remnant of an extensive tramroad system running between Coleford and Monmouth, disused now for well over a century but one of the earliest tramroads in England when developed nearly two hundred years ago. At Lower Lydbrook and Bishopswood the grassy terraces above the Wye are the bed of another old tramroad system which once meandered up into the slades and wooded valleys above the river.

Dean has seen many other industries. Still important is stone-quarrying; large quarries remain active near Coleford and in the Wye Valley south of Tintern, smaller ones survive in many parts of the Forest. At Cannop Ponds a remarkable little stoneworks still survives and thrives, cutting and blocking sandstone and limestone for use throughout Britain. A different use for stone was developed west of the Wye on the heights of Penallt Common where outcrops of quartz conglomerate, known as "Pudding Stone", were quarried and shaped into millstones for use in cornmills and cider presses.

These millstones often found their way abroad, acting as ballast in coastal trading ships. There's a pub beside the harbour at Bristol called the Llandoger Trow. The name recalls busy times when trows – a particular design of sailing ship – from Llandogo, well up the Wye, were a common sight in Bristol, on coastal routes and even, it is said, trans-atlantic trade routes. Ship building, on a small scale, once employed hundreds of people in Chepstow and Newnham, Brockweir and Monmouth. Many of even the smaller streams, or Pills, which flow from the Forest into the Severn once hosted tiny boatbuilding concerns. The Severn & Wye Railway and Canal Company developed a relatively small but thriving docks at Lydney through which to export the Forest's coal and ore; the Great Western Railway built smaller docks at Bullo Pill, near Newnham, for the same purpose.

From gold mining (Wigpool) to glassmaking (May Hill), wireworks (Tintern) to wood-distillation (for industrial alcohols, Cannop), extraction of ochre (for the paint industry, Clearwell) to paperworks (Whitebrook), the natural resources of the land of Dean have served man in myriad guises. New industries replace old, and tourism is now one of the area's most important employers. Today's Forest is, increasingly, a playground of woodland walks and bridleways, fishing ponds and picnic sites, activity centres and, above all, a desirable and increasingly expensive place to live.

The pithead winding gear is stilled and gone, only distant echoes remain. No longer does it rain black rain, nor the sky yellow with sulphur, nor brooks run red with waste. Today's Forest is green, clean and of a new generation. But prise open the years and the past is still there, a safe, fascinating but slowly fading shadow.

Catch it while you can.

The Freeminers

On a number of the walks in this book you'll encounter evidence of small scale coal mining activity. It may be no more than a seemingly pointless boarded up hole in a hillside beside a pile of dark shale, little larger than a farmyard muck-heap and all but hidden by encroaching brambles and bracken, rosebay willowherb and columbine. Nearby are a few rusting oildrums, lumps of aggregate, a rotting armchair, coils of rusting wire and decaying hausers snaking off into the undergrowth. The odd length or two of rail lie decaying beside decomposing sleepers sharply coloured by yellow and orange fungi. The whole has an air of being long-abandoned.

On the other hand you may stumble on a narrow tramroad crossing a forest track which, if followed, leads into a small shaft plunging down into the earth at an alarming angle. On the surface is a small hut housing a winch, the hauser from which follows the track beneath the guarding iron or wooden gates and down into the darkness. A couple of short sidings built on heaps of spoil carry small metal trucks along to a loading chute, the whole area is powdered by a covering of grey dust.

Either way, you've come across a freeminer's former or current place of work. Freeminers are something of an anachronism, but one which Dean is proud to host. Indeed they are an essential part of the Forest, one of the elements which combine with other less easily definable factors to give character to the area. They are of ancient calling, claiming an ancestry back to at least the time of the Romans in England, and are both the antecedents of and successors to the large scale mining industry dead these past 27 years in Dean.

Freeminers have the right to dig for and extract coal (and also iron ore, ochre and stone) from the Forest, in theory without hindrance and anywhere within the bounds of the Forest that they choose to work. In practice they are subject to self-imposed laws which regulate their undertakings, some of which laws date back to the middle ages. The Freeminers Court thus established exercises jurisdiction over all manner of disputes between actual or potential freeminers and is solely responsible for agreeing the licences, or grants, to enable a claimant to establish a working.

These grants are termed "gales" and are conferred by The Gaveller, the chief officer of the Forest and the Crown's representative, for the particular part of Dean concerned (there are two Gavellers, one for East Dean, one for West).

This is an ancient position harking back to the days of the Saxon and Norman kings who laid claim to vast tracts of lands in England for use as hunting demesnes by themselves and their favourites. Strict laws, in addition to the common law of the day, were enforced in these areas, the Gaveller's position derives from these times. So long as a claimant's favoured spot doesn't interfere with a pre-existing mine or gale, and the claimant satisfies the strict conditions by which he qualifies to be a Freeminer, then the Gaveller grants the gale to the applicant. Freeminers

Courts were once held at St. Briavels Castle, the residence of the Constable of the Forest, nowadays the less august offices of the Forestry Commission in Coleford house the Gaveller. Once a gale holder ("galee"), the Freeminer pays to the Crown a nominal annual rent plus a royalty on each ton of coal (ore, ochre or stone) raised.

To be eligible to be a Freeminer the applicant must be over 21 and have been born within the Hundred (an ancient measure of land) of St. Briavels, reside within that area, be both a freeman and son of a freeman and to have worked for a year and a day in one of the Forest's coal or iron mines.

At the height of Dean's industrial phase there could have been several thousand eligible claimants; as the industry died out, however, the numbers dwindled. Today maybe only a couple of hundred Freeminers hold the award of a Gale, of these just a handful work full-time in their tiny mines ... and highly lucrative they can be.

To some of the remainder it must be little more than an energetic hobby, pursued at weekend or on summer evenings. Yet others let out their Gales to outsiders, ensuring that the tradition remains an active practice. These galees, full time, part time or absentee, maintain and sustain a unique right of passage which goes back to time immemorial.

This long history has often brought the miners into conflict with "The Authorities" in the past, particularly with regard to the cutting of timber to provide pit props.

When taken into consideration along with the great amounts of timber cut by charcoal burners and by others who had purchased from the Crown rights of Assart (clearing small chunks or swathes of the Royal Forest), then the loss of immature woodland (that favoured by these croppers) occasionally reached crisis proportions. As one of the main functions of the Forest was to provide timbers for the English navy, then the destruction of much of the slow-growing hardwoods prematurely was cause for concern.

Thus during the reign of Good Queen Bess in 1565, for example, the cropping of trees was outlawed. Similar bans and/or restrictions were imposed on a number of occasions during the following centuries (and had been before, during the reign of Henry VIII for example). In 1838 a charge was imposed for the first time on the use of timbers for pit props under the terms of The Dean Forest Mines Act.

This, and a later Act of 1904, confirmed in law the rights and privileges of the Freeminers which had developed, piecemeal and as a function of tradition rather than right, during the previous millenium.

During Dean's great industrial phase the Freeminers didn't disappear, for it was only through them that the major coal, iron and ochre mines could be licensed. Thus the biggest mines and pits, such as Shakemantle Iron Mine or Princess Royal Colliery, would each be based on the grant of a gale to a true-born Freeminer, who then leased his option to a Foley, a Crawshay or whoever. The small-scale mining evident today was only put on hold during the Industrial Revolution, not subsumed by its developments.

Some of the free mines have been in continual operation for decades – in Howler's Slade, east of Broadwell for example, where a long established mine is visible from the main road – whilst others may be working on one visit but boarded up and abandoned on the next, only to have risen like a phoenix on a subsequent inspection.

The area to the north and west of Cannop Ponds and that to the south of Blackpool Bridge are the most likely places to find a gale being worked. Be cautioned, however, that they are working industrial sites, with all the attendant dangers, and they are private property, so don't trespass without permission.

Most galees welcome curious visitors, however, and such sites are well worth seeking out. The abandoned sites should be treated with all the respect due to the potential dangers of any old extractive industry, large or small. The vast majority of old shafts or adits (levels driven at varying angles into the valleysides) are sealed off, infilled or gated, but even so the undergrowth may still hide long-forgotten workings, so exercise caution!

Settlements

The area covered in this volume is dotted with towns, villages and hamlets, some of which pre-date the Roman invasion of these Islands whilst others are products of a much more recent revolutionary change, the Industrial Revolution. Where appropriate, the smaller towns and villages are described in relevant chapters; the larger ones richly deserve a separate section to themselves.

Monmouth

This is internationally recognised as one of the oldest and most historic towns in Britain. Its strategic site, at the confluence of the rivers Monnow and Wye, was appreciated by the Romans who established a military settlement, Blestium, to control this, one of the natural gateways into (or out of) South Wales. It developed in tandem as a commercial centre, becoming an important location for smelting iron dug from Dean; Cinderhill Street takes its name from this practice, although this name is the only reminder, the cinders having been removed several centuries ago for re-smelting elsewhere. Roman roads, albeit ill-defined, converge on the town and it seems likely that the Wye was used as a trade route to the sea beyond Chepstow.

There's little doubt that prior to the Romans, a Celtic people lived between the rivers, but evidence is slight. The Clawdd Du (Black Ditch) defensive line in Overmonnow may have pre-Roman origins, a tumulus near Dixton church almost certainly does, whilst the names of surrounding hills held in local usage – Grist Castle Hill, Buckholt Castle Hill – suggest an ancient lineage for this southern part of the old Kingdom of Archenfield which survived into the Dark Ages.

The Normans, as ever, left their mark. A few walls and ditches on a low river-cliff above the Monnow are all that remain of Monmouth Castle, birthplace of the Plantagenet King, Henry the Fifth, in 1387. Unique (in Britain at least) is the fortified bridge, Monnow Gate, at the southern end of Monnow Street; scant remains of another of the old town gates and a short section of town wall remain behind the Nag's Head pub off St. James's Square. Laying claim to be the oldest building in town is St.

Peter's Church at Dixton, beside the Wye to the northeast of the town, early Norman but with a Saxon foundation, closely followed by St. Thomas's at Overmonnow, beside the fortified gateway and which retains many early Norman features. As old as these buildings are the pastures now used by the town's sports clubs; Chippenham Meadows (or Meade) are the old common land of the Borough used, even in Elizabethan times, by townsfolk in "Tyme out of mynde" without hindrance (on payment of a nominal sum to the Manor/Burgesses) for the grazing of livestock on these floodmeadows between the town, the Wye and the Monnow.

Continuing the religious theme is the old Priory, near St. Mary's Church. Parts of it may date back to the Twelfth Century. The picturesque oriel, "Geoffrey's Window", is named after Geoffrey of Monmouth, a medieval historian who may have once been a Brother at this Benedictine Priory. His "Chronicon sive Historia Britonum" (Chronicles of the History of Britain), a sort of medieval version of "1066 and All That," sought to trace the lineage of the Kings of Britain, linking, for example, Alfred, Arthur and Merlin with King Lear and Cymbeline. Whilst his historical exactitude may be questionable, his influence on, for example, Shakespeare, Tennyson and Milton are undoubted. The Priory, overlooking the old town racecourse in a bend of the Monnow, is now a Youth Hostel.

The odd building survives from late medieval times, the Queen's Head, The King's Head and the Beaufort (now converted into flats but retaining its coaching yard, stables, etc.) for example, and vestiges of timber-framed buildings survive in the structure of a number of the buildings in Monnow Street.

Much of present day Monmouth, however, dates from Georgian times, and a large number of both grand and humble houses remain, many of them fronting the Norman/medieval street pattern which survives remarkably intact, centred on the Shire Hall (built in 1724 on the site of the old market house), so-named as the town was, until 1939, the administrative centre for the old County of Monmouthshire; the County Agricultural Show is still held here each last Thursday in August. Here, too, are statues to those local worthies Henry V and Charles Rolls, who was born and lived near Rockfield, two miles NW of Monmouth. The most impressive area of period housing is on and around St. James's Square, east of St. Mary's churchyard.

The A40 dual carriageway relieved the town of much traffic congestion, but also relieved it of surviving vestiges of former industries connected with the Wye; remains of old wharves and shipyards (ships up to 500 tons were built here) now lie beneath the road near the Wye Bridge traffic lights.

Gone too is the railway, the town once boasted two stations and a halt. One station was Monmouth Troy, named after the massive mansion, Troy House, which stands beside the little River Trothy a mile south of the town. Today a special school, it was once one of the homes of the Beaufort Family (of Badminton House fame); they also had built the Great Castle House (next to the castle). Some of the town's old corn mills still survive, derelict ones such as Mitchel Troy and Dixton, or as private houses such as Osbaston (near to which still stands the old municipal electricity works, complete with weir across the Monnow).

The museum in Priory Street is worth a visit, the local collection holds many relics and photographs of the town's history and industries whilst the adjoining Nelson Museum is dedicated to that renowned Admiral. He has only the most tenuous of connections with the town but a local admirer of his, Lady Llangattock, put together, during Victorian times, a formidable collection of artefacts (not including eyepatches or glass eyes...) later presented to the Town.

There's also a fascinating and long-term archaeological dig taking place in the premises of a former agricultural merchant's warehouse in Monnow Street, just downhill from Lloyd's Bank, which is open to the public.

The Tourist Information Centre is in the Shire Hall in Agincourt Square.

Chepstow

The old part of Chepstow tumbles steeply down from the Portwall, the old town wall, to the banks of the Wye which curves gracefully between high limestone cliffs en route to its confluence with the Severn just south of the town. Three manmade features dominate this gorge: Rennie's cast-iron roadbridge dating from 1816, an early example of such a structure; the spectacular railway bridge originally built by Isambard Kingdom Brunel for the South Wales Railway in 1852 (now largely hidden from view by the adjoining new relief road bridge); and the stone edifice of Earl FitzOsbern's massive castle. The first of the great Marcher castles, it was built from the outset (1067) in stone – as such it is the first stone-built castle in Britain – and remained garrisoned until 1695.

From it, William FitzOsbern, one of the three Marcher Lords, controlled – or attempted to – much of South Wales and the southern Marches; the many hundreds of smaller stone or motte & bailey castles in this vast area were built at his sufferance and owed total allegiance to him and his successors.

Aside from the fortified old town gateway, few medieval buildings remain, Hocker Hill being the nearest thing to a survival from that era although the underlying street pattern remains intact, a warren of narrow streets and walkways lined with old cottages, inns and merchants houses leading to the old port situated between the two bridges.

A few waterside warehouses still see use, though not from waterborne traffic. One unlikely export was the Chartist's leader John Frost who, with fellow leaders of the movement, was transported to Tasmania by the authorities in 1840; their prison ship sailed from Chepstow, a plaque near The Boat Inn records the event.

The town was once a major transhipment centre for goods brought down the Wye from as far upstream as Hay, nearly 100 watermiles away, on shallow-draught trows for transfer to seagoing vessels at Chepstow. The museum on Bridge Street records these times.

The priory church of St. Mary's is worth seeking out for its decorated tombs, including that of Henry Marten, one of the judges at the fateful trial of Charles I after the Second Civil War and signatory of his death warrant. The rest of this major Benedictine Priory, never completed, was rased to the ground at the dissolution of the monasteries in the 1530s.

The Tourist Information Centre is in the old gatehouse on High Street.

The Forest Towns

The industries that ravaged Dean in centuries past also created and nurtured many of the townships in today's Forest. **Cinderford** is almost entirely a creation of the Industrial Revolution, a ribbon of industrial villages and hamlets in the valley of the Cinderford Brook, stretching from Drybrook in the north to Soudley in the south, which coalesced to form essentially one long town, characterised by terraced housing, non-conformist chapels and haphazard development on incursions made into the woodland.

The first coke-fired iron furnace was developed in 1795 near Ruspidge, starting an iron-related industrial history which lasted until the last furnace in the town closed in 1894. Some of the related foundries, casting works, wireworks, engineering concerns and suchlike which sprang up in the valley survived until the Second War.

The extractive industries also attracted many people to the area. At its height perhaps a dozen or more coal and iron ore mines employed several thousand. The iron mines were all gone by 1900, the largest colliery, Lightmoor, just west of Ruspidge, closed in 1940; the last in the Forest, Northern United, northwest of Cinderford, on Christmas Day 1965. Nearly all traces of such heavy industry are now gone, recalled only in street and pub names, the character of the housing stock and the scattered scars of industrial wasteland as-yet awaiting reclamation.

Coleford too, is largely a product of past industry, although it does also have a few older buildings – the old manor house at Poolway, just north of the centre, for example, dates back to the Sixteenth Century and offered sanctuary to King Charles I, on the run from the battle of Edgehill in 1642. There are also some interesting, imposing buildings along Newland Road, en route to Whitecliff, as well as the folly building, Rock Castle.

If anywhere is the "Capital" of Dean then this is it (although the original administrative centre of Dean was always St. Briavels, a few miles to the SW).

It has a market charter dating from 1661 although the last market per se was held in 1946 on the sloping marketplace, now little more than a traffic island. The lone tower now here was built in 1821 as part of the parish church, St. Johns, the body of it was demolished in 1882; the old market hall shared the site and a similar fate, albeit in 1968.

Coleford's fortunes were founded on iron and stone; the western arm of the iron ore-bearing rocks bracket Coleford and were worked from earliest times (pre-Roman) until 1945 when the Old Ham mine near Clearwell (SW of Coleford) finally closed. The area was dotted with furnaces and forges, the sole survivor of which is at Whitecliff, just SW of the town centre where the substantial remains of the coke-fired furnace are protected as a Scheduled Monument.

One of the earliest of Dean's railways, the Monmouth Tramroad, in 1813 linked Coleford with the Wye navigation at Redbrook, offering an invaluable outlet for pig-iron produced in the local furnaces and forges.

There was even a local steel industry, developed in the 1840s, by the renowned metallurgist Robert Mushet at a site near Darkhill, south of Coleford and christened the Titanic Steel Works. This provided not only top grade steel (beloved of Sheffield craftsmen, to which city much was transported) but also the opportunity for Mushet to experiment with various steel alloys, later invaluable to the great steel industry of South Wales in the Twentieth Century. Like its namesake forty years later, the Titanic sank virtually without trace in 1871.

Many large quarries, working and abandoned, crater the landscape around the town, from which fine sandstones, limestones and Forest Bluestone have been exported to the four corners of the realm. One unusual industry which briefly flourished in Coleford was silk throwing (which sounds like it should be a pub sport), employing up to eighty persons in the 1830s.

The Tourist Information Centre is just off the Market Square.

Lydney has the longest history of the Forest towns; the Romans shipped iron ore from here (Lydney Pill), and relaxed in nearby Lydney Park where the extensive remains of a Roman Temple, dedicated to Nodens, a pagan god of healing and water, have been exposed and excavated.

The town straddles the old Roman road between Glevum (Gloucester) and Striguil (Chepstow) at a point on higher ground above an important ferry-crossing of the Severn, about 2 miles from the river; it also marks the end of the strategic trade route they developed through the spine of the Forest from Ariconium (near Ross).

Centuries later, the town was a cradle of the early charcoal-iron industry in Elizabethan times; the only buildings remaining from those times are Naas House, built on a shelf of higher ground a stone's throw from the expanses of the Severn's shifting sandbanks, and the much earlier St. Mary's Church which dates back to at least the Thirteenth Century.

A combination of railway and canal helped make the town's fortune in the Nineteenth Century. The railway funnelled timber, coal, stone and ore down from the Forest pits and quarries to great interchange sidings at Lydney Junction, south of the town on a "greenfield" site, from where it was transferred either by rail or by ship from the Lydney Docks, Harbour and Canal complex, built by the Severn and Wye Railway Company in 1813.

Tinplate works, foundries, furnaces, shipbuilding and sawmills developed in tandem, establishing the town's central role in the Forest's economy which it retains to this day (albeit with a rather different industrial base), exemplified by the large industrial estate which has been developed at the old docks and harbour.

1. The Monnow Valley

Route: Newcastle – White House – Skenfrith – Llanrothal – St. Maughans

Distance: 9 miles

Map: O.S. Pathfinder Sheet 1087

Start: The Wellington Inn, Newcastle. G.R. SO 173447

Access: Newcastle is a hamlet some six miles NW of Monmouth. Take the B4233 from Monmouth to Rockfield and go right at the junction in this village along the B4347; Newcastle is three miles along this road.

Wild mink, otters and kingfishers add spice to this challenging walk between the Monnow Valley's old castles and churches. Take a walking stick between June and September to demolish troublesome undergrowth in parts!

The Wellington Inn (060084 636)

For all but a handful of years around the turn of this Century, this picturesque old building has been an inn since its foundation in the Fifteenth Century. Old records show that it was The King's Arms until the close of the Napoleonic Wars when the commander of the local militia, one Captain Evans, persuaded the incumbent landlord to rename it in honour of the victor at Waterloo.

A small modern extension fits uncomfortably on one side of the pub which is otherwise an outstanding example of an old village local (not that there is much of a village), complete with public bar, a rare survival in these days of the gentrification and commercialisation of the country pub.

This bar drips with assorted artefacts redolent of the days of yore of yesterday's farms and various oddities such as an ancient spear from an obscure African tribe. The other bar houses the more usual selection of brasses, stuffed fish, prints and photos.

Two things you just can't miss are the pub plant and the pub dog. The plant, beneath which the building all but disappears in May, is a Wisteria, held to be the oldest in England and Wales. May is when the main flowering occurs, a veritable Niagara of violet blooms, but some secondary flowering persists throughout the summer. If you're not there in May then there are ample photographs in the pub which do some justice to the plant.

The pub dog is called Toby, a rather large Jack Russell. You'll find him scootering round the pub on his set of wheels, imported from the U.S.A. to give him his mobility back following severe arthritis and an unhappy puppyhood. He's part of the furniture at the Wellington now, but with no less than seven pub cats to contend with, maybe he's met his doggy Waterloo!

The Wellington opens noon to 2.30 p.m. except Mondays, and 7 p.m. to 11 p.m. (10.30 Sundays); there's a good selection of bar snacks and a separate restaurant section is open at weekends. The real ale on offer is Draught Bass, very occasionally augmented with (or replaced by) an alternative choice.

The Walk

Before leaving Newcastle, pop down the lane beside the pub for a few yards to gain a view of the considerable motte (mound) of the old motte and bailey castle from which the village takes its name. You can see it through a gap in the fence on your left just below the barn, the tree-covered motte is part of the farmyard of Newcastle Farm.

Return to the main road and turn left, the building next to the Wellington was once an endowed school used by the children of this scattered community. In about a quarter mile turn right along the "No through road" just before the white cottage and follow this to its end. Fine views open out to the right down the lower Monnow valley, well

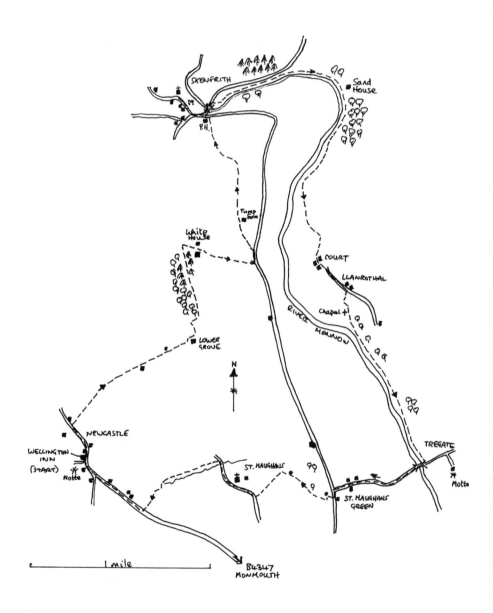

wooded and overshadowed at the far end by The Kymin, above Monmouth.

On reaching Lower Grove Farm bear left along the rough track which skirts the garden, then go left through the wide gap as this track bends right, around the barn. Follow this wide swathe to the foot of the slope then dog-leg right, then left and walk up the field road alongside the woods.

On reaching the top turn right along the surfaced road, walking behind White House Farm, continuing along the driveway beyond. Much of this lane was a part of the Hilston Park estate, the grand estate house, best seen from St. Maughans, near the end of the walk, has most recently seen use as a children's home.

Turn left along the road at the end, and left again about fifty yards further along, up the driveway to Tump Farm. Pass immediately to the left of the house, following the rough track to the far-right corner of the paddock where a well hidden step-stile gives access to the steep field beyond. Angle very slightly left up across this field, aiming to meet the fence along the top at a point about twenty yards to the right of the line of electricity poles.

Pausing for breath here, look behind over the flat-bottomed, steep-sided Monnow valley and up the side valley opposite, beyond the top of which you can see the round towers of Pembridge Castle, a fortified manor house, one of several in the district which remain private houses to this day.

Climb the stile and bear half left, soon cresting the narrow ridge top and unveiling glorious views up the valley of the Monnow, across to the distinct profiles of The Skirrid and The Sugar Loaf and the length of the Black Mountains. Below, the tiny village of Skenfrith nestles, curiously, on the outside of a meander (bend) of the Monnow, dominated by the old castle ruins.

Find the stile over the fence (about 70 yards above-left of the house) and scramble down the very steep, thistle-covered pasture, aiming roughly for the bottom-right of the field. Near this corner cross the old stile and continue downhill, aiming for the right of the white building at the slope's foot. The path reaches a minor road here, turn left and walk to The Bell Inn, beside the old river bridge here in Skenfrith. The onward route lies across the bridge, but allow ample time to experience the delights both of The Bell and of the village.

The castle is the most obvious feature, the curtain walls enclosing a central, circular keep. Until the early 1960s this was all that was known of the castle, but excavations begun then have revealed more and more of the many ancillary buildings within the defensive walls. The castle was one of the Trilateral Castles of Gwent, stone-built to impress upon the rebellious Celts of the area that the Normans meant business, and recognised that this area of northern Gwent was the most important route through the low hills of this part of the Marches.

It was built in about 1200 and, in common with the two other Trilateral castles at nearby Grosmont and Llantilio (White), was in the charge of Hubert de Burgh, a favourite of King John. The great green in front and at one side marks the line of the infilled moat, on a third side the Monnow was the moat and a fourth is now occupied by the Castle Mill. This still uses its waterwheel (visible from near the war memorial) to power machinery and grind corn, but is not open to visitors.

The other old building in the village is the splendid St. Bridget's Church, dating from much the same time as the castle. The squat tower is topped by a dovecote whilst the spacious, stone-flagged interior houses a great number of delights including wall paintings, a minstrels box, the splendid family pew and relief tomb of the Morgan family, one-time Lords of the Manor, and a spectacular survival of a medieval embroidered cope (cloak) [protected from damaging sunlight behind the green drapes near the Morgan tomb; re-draw the curtains when you've looked at the garment].

Return to the Bell Inn, cross the bridge and go right, over the stile at the footpath signposted for Broad Oak Road. The path soon joins the river bank and remains with it for a considerable distance, occasionally waymarked with yellow arrows. The copious blue wild flowers are Meadow Crane's Foot which seem to attract a lot of dragon and damsel flies. This is an excellent place to watch for buzzards, the woodland off to the left supports several pairs.

Cross the foot of the garden of the massive new "Sand House" and continue along the riverbank through the woods beyond. This stretch may be particularly difficult to negotiate during the summer as the thick

St. Bridget's Church, Skenfrith

undergrowth is head-high and the path not well used. Perseverance, however, brings you to more open fields as the valley floor opens out again.

Stick with the riverbank to the end of the second field (which may be under crops, the stile out of it is about 30 yards up along the hedge). The third field (which has an electricity pylon near the far-right corner) may also be blocked by crops. You need to get to the far top-left of this field (the stile half way down the far side, the official path, has been removed). Once here, climb the gate here and walk along the track to the farmyard gate. Continue through the long farmyard here at Llanrothal Court and along the surfaced road beyond. Just before reaching the white bungalow on your left, go through the gate on the right and walk round the edge of the field, through the gates to the isolated church.

This little chapel is all that remains of what has tentatively been recognised as the site of a village abandoned in medieval times; an old weir below the churchyard suggests a long-gone mill site, shards of pottery have been found and crop-marks visible in aerial photographs are evidence of former buildings.

Dedicated to St. John The Baptist and dating back to the early 1200s, it's now in the care of the Redundant Churches Fund. There's only access to half of it, simply, almost puritanically furnished with old, moveable wooden pews/settles, a carved pulpit and an ancient altar. The other half, visible through small windows on the south side, is totally unrestored. Inside the porch are a few old photographs offering a tantalising glimpse of the old church before its partial restoration.

The village it once served seems to have disappeared around 1400 A.D., too late to be a plague village (the Great Plague of 1348-9 which decimated the population and led to countless villages and hamlets being abandoned), more likely a victim of a long series of wet, sunless summers which affected northern Europe and with which medieval agriculture just could not cope. It is said locally that it was in the Parish of Llanrothal, and maybe at this very church, that the last recorded open use of the Latin Mass was delivered and celebrated, about 150 years after the Reformation.

Leave the somewhat overgrown churchyard via the gap/remains of a stile at the middle of the southern wall and follow the river downstream, crossing the stile beneath the great willow tree then tackling gates as necessary. The Monnow is one of Britain's cleanest rivers and this quiet, isolated stretch is still home to otters, though you'll be extremely fortunate to see one. Until the 1960s an active pack of Otter Hounds helped the river keepers control this supposed menace. Mink also make a home here and there's a good head of kingfisher and heron; despite all of these trials, however, you'll see some massive trout swimming lazily against the current, and the river also has a good run of salmon in the autumn.

The easiest place to see the salmon is as they leap up weirs, there's an old one of these just below Tregate Bridge, at which point the walk joins a minor road. Before you cross the bridge note the massive old motte beside Tregate Farm, just above the valley floor downstream of the bridge. The bailey is also discernible, and the castle's old fishponds have been recognised by authorities on the subject. A back road runs through the site, but you won't see too much unless you know what you're looking for.

Cross Tregate Bridge and follow the road up to the hamlet of St. Maughan's Green. Bear left at the junction and in a few yards right, across the cattle grid and down the surfaced driveway. Within ten yards a waymark arrow points left to a stile in the hedge, once over which turn right and descend to the footbridge in the bottom corner of the field. Beyond this, keep the hedge to your right 'till the first ash tree, then angle slightly left up the field and head towards the old barn which soon comes into view, reaching this via a precarious crossing of the steep-sided brook.

This old barn turns out to be an abandoned cottage, now re-roofed and used as a byre. Remarkably, many of the cast-iron fittings remain in situ, albeit rusting away. Still there are the old firegrates, the range, the bread oven and even an old spike from which to hang pots or kettles over an open fire.

Don't cross the stile just beyond the ruin, instead turn left, upfield, and head for the top hedge at the point where the line of pylons crosses it.

Climb the stile here and turn right along the back lane to reach St. Maughans Church.

The church dates largely from the Thirteenth Century and was restored, to an extent, in 1863 by the Rolls family who owned virtually all the land in the area; a scion of the family, who lived at the massive Hendre mansion near Rockfield, was Charles Rolls, early aviator and co-founder of the famous motor car manufacturers. The church, and the hamlet it serves, takes its name from St. Meugan, one of the seemingly endless supply of Celtic saints after which many churches of the western side of Great Britain are named. The most obvious feature inside are the massive timber pillars holding up the barrel-vaulted roof, they are nearly 600 years old, having replaced the original stone ones when the church was wasted by Owain Glyndwr during his bloody campaign against Henry's IV and V. As at Skenfrith, the tower is capped by a wooden dovecot.

From St. Maughans Church go right, down the narrow lane to the stream and take the signposted footpath on the left. This leads to a series of recently repaired/replaced stiles which take the path gradually uphill along the line of the stream, passing through both cultivated fields and a glorious hay meadow resplendent with myriad colourful flowers in late spring and summer, including tall, yellow Agrimony and blue/purple Bellflowers.

At one point, the path dog-legs to the left through an overgrown, marshy hollow before reaching the road, upon which turn right to Newcastle. The first building on the right that you pass was once the village's other pub, The Castle Inn, but this closed in the early 1960s.

2. White Castle

Route: Llantilio – Treadam – White Castle – Pantycollin

Distance: 5.5 miles

Map: O.S. Pathfinder Sheet 1086

Start: The Hostry Inn, Llantilio Crossenny. G.R. SO 396147

Access: Take the B4233 northwest from Monmouth (from the round-about immediately south of Monnow Bridge Gateway) and continue towards Abergavenny for about eight miles. The pub is signposted to your left off this road.

An easy walk along the Offa's Dyke Path and country lanes visiting an ancient church and a substantial Marcher Castle.

The Hostry Inn (060085 278)

This must be one of the oldest pubs in Wales, dating as it does from 1459. An aberration in Victorian times meant it was de-licensed for about 20 years, but other than this, it's been slaking the thirst of travellers, pilgrims and wayfarers since the Wars of the Roses. Its name is probably a corruption of "Hostelrie" as this unlikely setting was once a regular stop on the perambulations of his see made by the Bishop of Llandaff in medieval times, whilst he will have been lavishly entertained at the local manor many of his train must have been lodged in less grand establishments, or hostels. This was a common practice in pre-reformation days; indeed, the oldest continually licensed pub in Britain, The George at Norton St. Philip (Somerset), had a similar foundation.

Today's traveller is rewarded with a choice of the Bitter, Special and Pale Ale brewed by The Wye Valley Brewery in Hereford, a small concern with an excellent reputation. Certainly no complaints about the way these beers are kept at the Hostry, it was Gwent CAMRA Pub of the Year in 1992. Occasionally, other ales may replace one or more of these Bull Mastiff from a tiny brewery in Penarth for example.

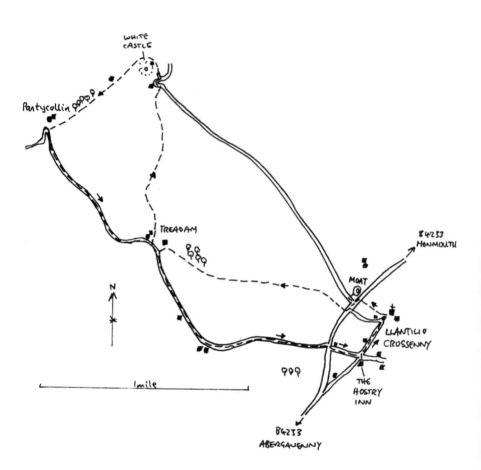

The pub has one or two architectural quirks. An adjoining medieval barn has recently been refurbished and now acts as a function room, the local folk club use it every fortnight for example. It doubles as a skittles alley. Down behind the main bar a steep staircase leads to an all-but hidden parlour, effectively doubling the capacity of the pub.

The pub is open from noon to 3 p.m. and 6 p.m. to 11 p.m., wide ranging bar snacks and meals on offer during both sessions. Children are welcome and, as the pub is on Offa's Dyke Path, there's no problem with the odd muddy boot or sodden cagoule!

The Walk

Bear right from the pub's door and walk downhill (i.e. not right again in front of the building), over the stream and through to the church, at the end of its cul-de-sac at the top of the hamlet. St. Teilo's Church dates largely from the 14th Century on a site first consecrated in around 550 A.D. The hamlet takes its name from this very early Bishop of Llandaff, all is explained in an informative leaflet which you can pick up in the church. The regular visits made by the Bishops of Llandaff help explain the great size of the church in proportion to the village, whose population will rarely have been much larger than it is at present.

Immediately to the left of the steps leading up into the churchyard a metal kissing gate gives access to a path which skirts the top end of a well manicured garden, exiting this at the far side and then continuing along the outside of the graveyard wall. At the corner of this wall continue straight ahead, roughly along the line of the electricity poles. Pass through the rather stiff kissing gate at the far side of the pasture and walk a few yards up the minor road opposite.

On the right here is a well-tended moated area, the sole remains of the old village manor house of Hen Gwrt, Welsh for "The Old Court". This was the likely home of one Sir David Gam, hero of Agincourt, whose family coat of arms is to be seen on the Hostry's pub sign. The deep moat is ablaze during spring and early summer with Yellow Flag Iris, keep an eye out, too, for frogs and newts.

Return to the main road and turn right, in a hundred yards or so go right with the Offa's Dyke Footpath signpost and commence the long, gentle climb through a series of large fields, following the obvious line of stiles. The horizon is formed by the distinct shape of the Skirrid mountain, just to the north of Abergavenny.

There's no evidence of any Dyke along this section of the Long Distance Footpath, indeed its route here is largely conjectural. It's generally accepted that the project was never completed, and whilst in some stretches the Dyke is spectacular and in others a natural feature such as a river acted as the defensive line, some sections of Offa's great scheme never left the proverbial drawing board. The Path seems to be routed here for its scenic grandeur rather than for any historical accuracy.

The stiles lead up to the copse on the hilltop ahead, a waymark arrow directs you along the left side of this to join a field road some yards this side of the imposing Georgian farmhouse of Great Treadam. Turn left along this and then right along the minor road. In 100 yards or so turn right along the back lane beside the cottage and, simply, remain with this for about a mile. This snakes up the hillside between high banks and hedges, an ancient routeway bedecked with meadowsweet, campion, fumitory and trefoil giving a great splash of colour throughout the summer. At one point a gateway allows glimpses of the view eastwards along the winding valley of the river Trothy towards distant Monmouth.

As the lane joins the minor road at the end bear left and then walk ahead along the No Through Road to reach White Castle. There is an entrance fee to visit this, the largest of the Trilateral Castles of Gwent (see also the Newcastle walk). It's a complex jigsaw of curtain walls, towers, ditches and moats, all reinforcing its commanding hilltop position from which are glorious views across to the Skirrid, the Sugar Loaf and the Black Mountains, views appreciated, if for differing reasons, by its builders over 800 years ago as well as today's ramblers.

The name White Castle is held to reflect the rather unexpected practice adopted by its defenders of whitewashing the fortress walls, presumably to add an extra psychological dimension to its dominating physical presence. It lasted barely 300 years as a functioning fortress, the pacification of the Welsh over several medieval centuries and the eventual Act of Union during Henry VIIIth's reign robbing it of any military function. By Elizabeth's reign it was a ruin. It's oft said locally that during the Second War Hitler's deputy, Rudolf Hess, was held for a time at a secure location in the locality, during the course of which he visited the castle on many occasions, passing a few countless hours by feeding wildfowl on the moats.

The Offa's Dyke Path is signposted along the track between the outer moat/ditch and the band of woodland. Follow this past the old cottage to the field gate and turn right down the field, heading for the barn in the bottom-right corner.

Here, ignore the Offa's Dyke path to the right and continue ahead, passing the barn on your right and following the edge of the field down alongside a deepening little valley. At the bottom of the next field the "stile" through the hedge appears to double as the guard rail over a water trough, so cross with care and continue downhill towards the farm in the valley below. Leave the bottom field virtually opposite this farm and turn left along the drive. In a few yards turn left along the minor road and follow this back to Llantilio about two miles away, going straight across at the crossroads to return directly to The Hostry.

The Hostry Inn, Llantilio Crossenny

(It's one of the great trials of researching a book such as this that such a walk should have to be completed along albeit quiet back roads when the local map shows miles of potentially excellent public footpaths which could make the walk even more enjoyable. Sadly, in this area of North Gwent, stiles are blocked off, barbed wire fences raised across footpaths, footbridges fallen and unrepaired and those paths which are still accessible largely unsignposted from highways. Many factors combine to produce this ruinous state of affairs, largely, perhaps, lack of resources and a general lack of interest on the part of both rambler and landowner alike. I've sent my comments to the appropriate local authority; if you come across similar problems in your own area then do the same, public footpaths are an all too rare resource these days.)

3. Coppet Hill

Route: Goodrich – Coppet Hill – Welsh Bicknor – Kerne Bridge

Distance: 9 miles

Start: The Cross Keys Inn, Goodrich Cross, G.R. 566190

Map: O.S. Outdoor Leisure Sheet 14, Wye Valley & Forest of Dean

Access: Goodrich Cross is on the the A40 Monmouth to Ross dual carriageway, one junction north (i.e. the Ross side) of the junction for Hereford and Goodrich Castle. The Cross Keys is immediately east of the overbridge.

Bus: A very infrequent service 61 runs, Mondays to Fridays only, between Ross and Monmouth, stopping at The Cross Keys.

Dramatic views and a peaceful riverside stroll through the Wye gorge combine with medieval buildings on a largely footpath-based walk also rich in wildlife interest.

The Cross Keys (0600 890650)

When built in the mid 1960s the dual carriageway obliterated the old coach road between Ross and Monmouth but fortuitously spared this old coaching inn, dating back over 300 years and founded not long after Goodrich Castle's last stand during the Civil War. The pub's resident lady ghost may date from this period, she's apparently regularly seen walking the corridors of the second floor.

Much more recently the Inn's old stables have been integrated into the lounge bar, explaining the peculiarly high ceiling and the odd doorway several yards above floor level, it's the entrance to the old hayloft. The bare stone walls drip with myriad artefacts including, strangely, a large number of saws and countless keys ancient and modern. An old upright piano nestles next to the massive open fireplace, itself decked with a collection of brass plates.

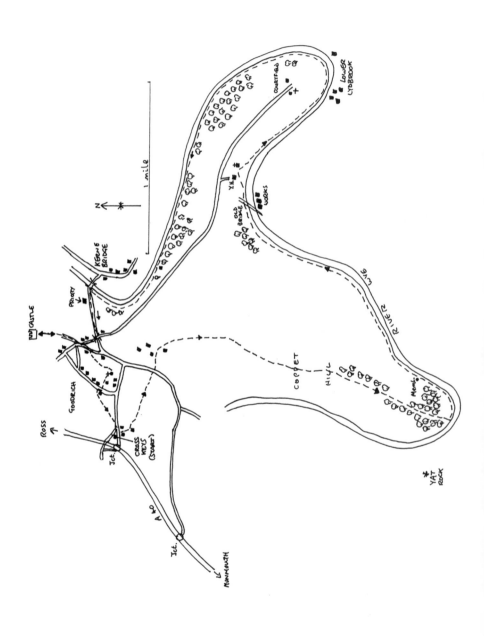

The Cross Keys retains a large public bar, replete with all the usual pub games; in addition there's a skittle alley alongside the beer garden at the rear of the old three-storey building. The beers on offer are from the Whitbread stable, Flowers Original and IPA in the lounge with further handpumps offering Boddingtons and draught cider in the public bar. Opening hours are 10.30 a.m. – 4 p.m. and 7 p.m. – 11 p.m., standard hours on Sundays. A wide selection of bar meals is available.

The Walk

Walk along the rough roadway opposite the Cross Keys (there's a footpath sign in the cupressor hedge) and on reaching Red Barn Cottage bear left this side of it, walking along the drive for a few yards. As the cupressor hedge on your left ends go through the narrow gap between this and the wooden-rail fence and turn right, then following the line of thorn hedge on your right along the field edge.

At the dogleg, continue ahead, this time with the hedge on your left, to reach a stile beneath an oak tree. Once over this walk ahead across the field to the next stile visible about fifty yards ahead, then walk down to the far bottom-right corner.

Cross the road here, (it's at a nasty bend so take your time), and walk up the rough lane opposite, continuing up the narrow, hedged pathway as the lane veers left. At the split in the path bear right and walk up past the telegraph pole to the rough lane at the top, going straight over this and then following the path beneath the line of pylons which strike diagonally up the side of Coppet Hill.

Having gained the main path just below the ridgetop, bear right with it and walk virtually due south along this surviving outcrop of Quartz Conglomerate rock. This helps give the Hill its distinct shape, considerably steeper on this western face than the eastern slope where the older, less erosion-resistant Lower Devonian sandstone predominates. Coppet Hill is common land, but this doesn't necessarily mean that you have the freedom to roam as this right is generally vested only in those who live in the immediate area. And on a purely practical point, it's much easier to stick to the well worn path as the thick growths of bracken, brambles and scrub conceal many small cliffs and short, sheer drops, a result of large boulders of the Quartz Conglomerate becoming detached from the steep slope in times past.

Views west from the path stretch over South Herefordshire to the dark wall that is the Black Mountains, across an undulating landscape of ridges and wooded hills dotted with tiny villages and ancient farmhouses. Ahead and to the right the thickly wooded slopes of Huntsham Hill and Coldwell sweep around in a graceful curve high above the Wye, here towards the top end of its famous gorge through which it meanders for nearly thirty miles to the Severn Estuary beyond Chepstow.

If your eyes are keen, you'll spot tiny figures crowded on the viewpoint that is Yat Rock; in every way the views you get from Coppet Hill are equally as dramatic and far-reaching – what you miss of Yat-Rock's view of the Malvern Hills to the north you gain through views to the Black Mountains to the west. Below the Rock, velcro-foundationed cottages cling to the side of the gorge amidst the trees and creepers.

Over the years the farmable, croppable east side of the common has been inclosed; the path skirts a series of such fields before gradually becoming entrapped by the woodland which envelops the southern tip of Coppet Hill. Initially, the woods are largely of coppiced hazels with the occasional birch, pine and Spanish chestnut but as the path falls downhill mature ash and oak come to dominate. Once free of this woodland walk ahead to the riverbank and turn left, upstream.

This is a dramatic section of the Wye Gorge, great pinnacles and abutments of dolomitic limestone standing free of or proud from the edge of the Dean plateau and thrusting above the great swathes of oak, beech, pine and yew woods. These inaccessible cliffs and spires are one of the relatively few places where Peregrine Falcons live and nest, their numbers having been decimated more than virtually any other bird of prey by the past actions of gamekeepers and the effects of pesticides. Another reason for their decline is said to be that their appetite for pigeon led to the loss of many encoded messages being ferried by carrier-pigeon during the Second War, in consequence a price was put on the peregrine's head!

Coldwell Rocks, Wye Valley

In a short distance the riverside path re-enters the woodland, vast ash trees and gnarled old chestnuts clinging to the ever-steepening slopes. Fortunately you remain at the foot of these slopes. In a quarter-mile or so you'll reach a memorial monument surrounded by rusting railings; it's quite easy to miss during the summer months when seasonal vegetation all but swamps it – it's on your left.

It recalls the death by drowning at this point, in September 1804, of one John Whitehead Warre; the inscription is a lengthy one which I'll leave you to discern at your leisure. Above the opposite bank of the Wye the line of firs marks the course of the old Wye Valley Railway which followed the gorge through cuttings and tunnels and across viaducts from Kerne Bridge to Chepstow, it closed in 1959.

Remain with the riverside path for the next two miles or so, casting an occasional glimpse behind to appreciate the conical-like shape of Rosemary Topping on the far bank. In summer the path is, in places, a defile trampled through huge fronds of bracken and stands of balsam, relief coming only when the woods are reached once again. The old railway viaduct beneath which you pass is now a part of the Wye Valley Walk footpath; on the far bank the large factory, now producing cardboard, was once an important cable works, manufacturing telephone wires and electricity cables amongst other things.

A little way beyond the viaduct the path splits just beyond a cottage, take the left fork and walk up to the substantial old vicarage at Welsh Bicknor, now a Youth Hostel. Pass in front of this to reach St. Margaret's Church, nestling in the trees and blessed with a small tower somewhat reminiscent of an Italian village church. The current church has been dated 1858, although many of the gravestones date back to the 1750s. The interior remains a mystery, I've never found it unlocked, but your luck may be better, apparently it contains spectacular stone-carving work. (n.b. The key isn't kept at the Youth Hostel). In the trees beside the church are the remains of a considerable old building.

Regain the riverside path and continue upstream. On the snout of the ridge to your left is a further small church, the focal point of a seminary run by the Mill Hill Fathers where future missionaries are trained, founded here by the Nineteenth Century churchman Cardinal Vaughan who was himself born here. Today it's an uncomfortable mixture of Georgian and 1960s buildings; its origins, however, are much older, here at Courtfield the young Prince Harry, later Henry V, spent most of his early years in the care of Lady Alice Salisbury. An old, roughly cobbled track once plunged down from here to a ferry across the Wye, still marked on inter-war maps but now long out of use.

A further good two miles of riverside path, much of it through pleasant woodland, brings you to Kerne Bridge, a splendid high-arched bridge of mellow sandstone. This former toll-bridge replaced another old ferry crossing of the Wye in around 1828.

Nearby is Flanesford Priory, now carefully (and award-winningly) rejuvenated as holiday apartments, until recently this old Augustinian Priory was largely in ruins or used as a barn and cattle byre. It was founded in 1347 and survived less than 200 years before succumbing to the reformist fervour of Henry VIIIth. It's one of a number of old structures in Goodrich, by far the most famous of which is Goodrich Castle, reached by following the road up left from Kerne Bridge, climbing the steps onto the overbridge at the top of the hill and going right, then right again at the Castle sign.

Dating from the early Twelfth Century and surviving until slighted by Parliamentarians during the Civil War, it's one of the most impressive of Marcher Castles, in a dominant hilltop position controlling the Wye to one side and several passes into Wales on another. It only fell after a long siege culminating in the use of a fearsome cannon christened Roaring Meg which fired cannonballs weighing 200lb at the structure and its defenders.

In 1828, in a bid to equal the castle's grandeur and setting, one Sir Samuel Meyrick had built, on the adjoining hilltop just northwest of the Castle, a great Gothic-style pseudo castle he called Goodrich Court, complete with baronial hall and gatehouses and furnished with all the trappings of mediaeval life – you know, suits of armour, shields, stuffed wolves and boars, that sort of thing. In fact, it's said that it was built solely for the purpose of housing the considerable collection of medieval armour Meyrick had amassed over the years.

It lasted little more than a century before being demolished in 1949; I recall reading, some years ago, that it was transported stone-by-stone to New England and reconstructed there, but I've never come across any corroborating evidence to support this. It certainly drew Wordsworth's scorn when he was progressing down the "Wye Tour" in the 1830s. A gatehouse remains, beside the A40 dual carriageway west of the village, which gives a taste of what the main house may have looked like. Derelict for a number of years, this structure was sold in the 1960s for a nominal sum (around £1 I believe) on the condition that the purchasers renovated and lived in the property.

Dating from the same time is Goodrich's other pub, The Hostelrie, another pseudo-Gothic edifice at the northern end of the village, dating from the same time as Meyrick's Court but based on a much earlier inn site; it's a hundred or so yards up the road to the right from the foot of the lane to the castle.

From the foot of this lane bear left along the main street and follow the main road south towards Whitchurch and Monmouth. Immediately past the school's lay-by a path leads, right, across the school playing field and through pastures to the parish church, St. Giles's. A past incumbent here was Thomas Swift, grandfather of Jonathan Swift, the author of, amongst other works, Gulliver's Travels. There's an unusual gravestone in the churchyard, in the 1880s one of the large boulders of quartz conglomerate fallen from Coppet Hill was moved to the graveyard and had a small concrete memorial slab inserted, in memory of two members of the Herbert family. There's also a grandiose tomb in the NW corner to Lucy, wife of the owner of Goodrich Court.

Leave the graveyard via the gate near this corner, passing beside the solid old white-painted yeoman's house and then up the rough drive beyond to a minor road. Turn right along this and walk the twenty or so yards to the right-hand bend. Here, look carefully on your left for the black-painted metal footpath gate leading into the corner of the left-hand field, there's also a well hidden footpath sign here. Walk along the edge of the field (garden to your left) for about thirty yards to the step stile, climb this and turn right, then follow the line of stiles, keeping the hedge/ditch on your right, to the minor road in front of the 1960s house. Turn right to return to the Cross Keys just a short distance away.

4. Buckholt

Route: Manson's Cross – Buckholt Wood – Welsh Newton – Newton Court

Distance: 10 miles

Map: O.S. Outdoor Leisure Sheet 14, Wye Valley & Forest of Dean

Start: The Royal Oak, Monmouth. G.R. SO 510145

Access: The Royal Oak is at the top of the Hereford Road in Monmouth, about a mile from the town centre. At the traffic lights past the Old Priory (the Youth Hostel beside St. Mary's Church) turn left up the A466 and follow this up the steep hill beneath the footbridge. The pub is on the right at the very crest of this hill.

Bus: Infrequent service 416, Mondays to Saturdays from Monmouth to Hereford

---

A long, easy walk mostly in woodland, following long forgotten roadways and visiting the grave of a Saint. The last 75 yards of the walk are scandalously overgrown and encroached on by garden hedges.

The Royal Oak (0600 772505)

A roadhouse dating from late Georgian times, the Oak probably originated as a staging point for coaches where horses could be exchanged or added depending on the direction of travel; the steep hills either side (south to Monmouth or north over the Buckholt) would require additional animals for hauling or braking.

Its lofty situation enjoys commanding views across to the heights of Dean, and down the wooded defile of the Wye as it re-enters its twisting gorge, immediately south of Monmouth. These are views best appreciated from the quiet beer garden behind the pub, beyond which pastures tumble to the local golf course. "An ideal location for the Nineteenth Hole" enthuses mine host, Doug, whose knowledge of the sport obviously stems from the *Nintendo* school of golfing.

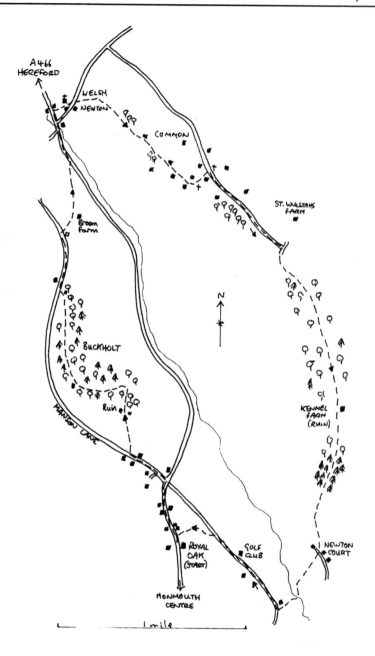

Or perhaps it's the fumes from the Flowers Original and Boddingtons Bitters currently available that so-affect his perception. The Oak has recently become a free house, shaking off the Whitbread tie of old, and further additions to the range of beers are threatened.

The pub essentially has one main room with a side room dedicated to pool and the other usual pub games; there's also a separate restaurant. Less formal culinary preparations come from the good selection of bar meals available daily; strangely the large tank of tropical fish aren't available as a catch your own "Poisson 'n Platter" option (good marketing ploy there, Doug...).

If the walk, the ales or the licensee's jokes don't drain you of energy there's also a skittles alley at the back of the pub. Opening hours are 11 a.m. – 3 p.m. and 5 p.m. – 11 p.m., all day Saturdays and standard hours on Sundays. Bar meals can be had until 10 p.m.

The Walk

Continue away from Monmouth along the main road and, in a quarter of a mile or so, turn left along Manson Lane here in the hamlet of Manson's Cross. The white house immediately past this turn, set at an angle to the road, is one of Monmouth's many lost pubs.

The lane winds gently up these southern slopes of Buckholt Hill, the wooded summit up to your right. At the crest of the hill a public footpath sign on the right points the way over a field gate to Buckholt Wood. Follow the line of the hedge on your right up a couple of fields to reach the old barn at the edge of the woods, pausing here to appreciate the views over Monmouth and, further to the west, the hills beyond the Vale of Gwent.

Pass to the right of the old barn and trace the path up through the woodland. Almost immediately on your right are the remains of one of a considerable number of cottages which once stood beside these age-old routeways, all now long abandoned and, in most cases, reduced to rubble. This gradual climb through pastures and the woodland edge is the most strenuous part of the whole walk. The climb ends as the path reaches a junction of forestry roads. Here turn left along the narrower green track in the direction of the "3" waymark arrow, a point of designation in a local walks leaflet.

The walk now follows this wide track along a terrace around the snout of Buckholt Hill, gaps in the trees here and there allowing glimpses across the Monnow Valley below. Ignore the waymark arrow to the left some distance later, instead continuing along the undulating track through the mixed woodland. There's a thick undergrowth of bracken which tends to keep the wildflower growth to a minimum but, on the plus side, there are plenty of woodpeckers, goldfinches and buzzard to keep an eye out for and a small herd of fallow deer make their home in these woods. Also in these woods you cross the border between Wales and England.

Not far past a small wooden hut the track issues onto a surfaced lane, turn right and walk uphill with this, soon passing by an old cottage, The Oldshop, on your left. Beyond this the trees retreat and sweeping views are revealed across the Monnow, far below, to the Black Mountains.

In about 200 yards is a badly overgrown old brick barn on your right. Immediately after this climb the small, rather overgrown gate on your right (there's a strand of barbed wire wrapped around it, but this is the public footpath) and walk diagonally across the large field, passing well above Broom Farm, down on your right. Once through the gate in this corner walk along the field road through two further pastures, emerging onto the A 466 in the valley bottom.

Turn left and follow this quite busy road along to Welsh Newton, no more than a hamlet of a few cottages and farms and distinctly lacking in the pub stakes. What it does have, however, is a smashing little old church. To reach it ignore the first turn right by the war memorial and continue up to the rough lane on the right which leads to the churchyard gate.

St. Mary's Church was founded by the Knights Templar in the 1200s, ·passing to the Knights Hospitaller a century later. These various sects were established to protect and aid pilgrims en route to and from the Holy Land. In time, their dedication to their original cause was usurped by greed for power and wealth and they were suppressed in the

Fourteenth Century. Quite what they were doing with foundations in the Marches is unclear, there are only a small number of their churches in Britain, many of them in this area. An excellent church leaflet outlines the points of interest, which include a fine stone Rood Screen, rarely found in a church of this size (if you're ever in the Peak District, compare it with the one at Chelmorton).

St. Mary's Church, Welsh Newton

This is also the unlikely resting place of a Saint, canonised earlier this century. John Kemble was the Catholic priest to the Kembles of Pembridge Castle (a fortified manor house which still stands two miles away), a tenuous position at the time (during and after the Civil War) as the religion was suppressed.

In one of the many witch-hunts such clergy suffered during the reign of Charles II, John Kemble was arraigned by Titus Oates as a being a member of a "Popish Plot" to kill Charles and his ministers in 1678. The eighty year old Kemble was sent to London to stand trial, was acquitted but returned to Hereford to further be tried as a practicing Catholic priest. Of this he was convicted and beheaded in August 1679, his body being brought to Welsh Newton for burial as he was locally born. His simple gravestone is still there, next to the churchyard cross.

Leave the large graveyard by the small gate to the east of the church (beneath a sycamore some yards up from the bungalow) and cross the pasture to the stile at the far side. Cross the lane here and the stile beyond, walking up the field to another stile. Continue up to a further stile, once over which bear half right to the offset corner (i.e. not the corner with the telegraph pole but the one 100 yards uphill from this), marked by an old metal cartwheel in the fence nearby. Climb the gate here and head across the field, roughly in line with the electricity wires. Whereas these pass to the left of the hilltop wood you should aim for the right, climbing the stile here and edging the woods over further stiles.

After the second stile (below a cottage) bear right along the edge of the horse pasture, cross a further stile and walk along the bottom of the rough field, aiming for the right of the red-tiled bungalow (if, by now, you're in woods then you've climbed the wrong stile out of the horse pasture). This direction brings you to an initially rough lane, follow it past a number of cottages and bend left, passing by the garage which acts as St. Faith's Church here at Welsh Newton Common. This lane ends at a T-junction, at which turn right.

At the time of writing a tiny old methodist chapel stands derelict at this junction, all but hidden behind overgrown laurels and trees. The door ajar, the pulpit still hanging from the wall, an old foot-operated organ supporting dusty, damp old prayer books and a Bible half filling the tiny interior, it may well have been sold for conversion by the time this is published. A melancholy find.

Having turned right, simply follow this newly resurfaced road to its end about half a mile further on. To the left, glimpsed through trees is St. Wulstan's Farm, recognised as the site of a Jesuit Xaverian Priory suppressed under the Reformation; a nearby copse is still known as Chapel Wood.

At the point the surfaced lane ends turn right and walk along to the woods. From this more open lane you get views across the plain the Wye has created in Herefordshire to The Malvern Hills and, nearer at hand, to Ross-on-Wye, Penyard Hill and the northern edge of Dean's plateau. Nearer still the bare hillside of Coppet Hill takes the eye to Yat Rock and the start of the Wye Gorge.

On reaching the woods just continue on along the main track into the trees, ignoring all turns or forks to left or right. This very old lane is lined by a succession of venerable old oaks, massive Spanish chestnut trees and occasional plane trees, almost certainly planted deliberately several centuries ago when this was a well used route from the heights of Welsh Newton to the important markets in Monmouth. For some of its length, it also marks the boundary between England and Wales.

A series of pastures on the left allow views to the dome-like hill of the Little Doward, its wooded crown of conifers planted with deciduous varieties and an evergreen species which spells out "E.R.", marking the date of planting as the coronation year of the present monarch.

The ruins of Kennel Farm, wreathed in knotweed, are the only ones along this section of the walk, rising from the undergrowth to your left and still surrounded by rough, unkempt pastures. A stretch of majestic beech trees accompanies the track to a stand of rather gloomy firs, just inside which bear right at the waymark arrow and start a long descent along the sunken, walled road which eventually winds up on the surfaced driveway of Newton Court, a large bay-fronted mansion a short distance to your left.

Go straight across this road and down the signposted footpath opposite, dropping the whole way down this sweeping slope to the sinuous, wooded course of Mally Brook. Ahead, Monmouth is at your feet. Cross the gate/tractor bridge across the water and look up half-right to sight the next stile beside a gate on the skyline. Once over this walk along the edge of the field, to the left of the house and to the surfaced lane.

Turn right up this, Manson's Lane, and follow it up past the newly extended golf clubhouse. Continue up the roughening lane to find a footpath sign on your left. Climb the stile here and the one a few yards across the ensuing pasture. Once over this head half-right to the corner of the substantial hedge and walk uphill with this on your left. Climb the stile in the corner here and force your way along this atrociously overgrown public footpath to the main road about 75 yards distant, emerging just yards from the Royal Oak.

5. The White Brook

Route: Penallt – Whitebrook – New Mills – Penallt Common

Distance: 5 miles

Map: O.S. Outdoor Leisure Sheet 14, Wye Valley & Forest of Dean

Start: The Bush Inn, Penallt. G.R. SO 522093

Access: Penallt is about four miles south of Monmouth along minor roads off the B4293 road to Trellech. Follow this road from Monmouth, bear left at the junction just south of the town marked by a white-painted old toll house, climbing steadily up to the plateau. Penallt is signposted along the first road on the left, about half a mile after the severe double bends. At the crossroads in the village turn left, then fork right at the war memorial along the rough track to the Green.

A walk full of interest for the industrial archaeologist. One long, potentially very muddy descent, one short, steep climb, the walk is largely on forest paths and quiet back-roads.

The Bush Inn (0600 772765)

Penallt village was a publess zone for around a year before The Bush Inn reopened in July 1992. The new owners have completely gutted and redesigned the centuries old building, resulting in a large open-plan layout partially sub-divided into distinct areas aimed at barflies, loungers and diners.

The glory of the resurrected pub must be the terrace at the rear, offering magnificent views down across adjoining pastures to the wooded mass of the Forest of Dean, lying at the far side of the unseen Wye Gorge; the distinctive tower of Newland Church stands proud of the trees in the middle distance. This large back garden also has play facilities (swings, etc.) for children. The beers on handpump are Bass and Hancocks HB, available between 11.30 a.m. – 3 p.m. (4 p.m. on Saturdays, closed Monday lunchtimes) and 6 p.m. – 11 p.m., standard Sunday hours. Bar meals are available during most of these hours.

The Walk

Return to the war memorial and walk along the road away from it and back to the crossroads. Go straight across these along the road towards Tregagle and The Narth and, in about thirty yards, bear left along the rather indistinct grassy path which, within yards, passes over an old cattle grid.

Climb the stile soon after and follow the surfaced driveway along through the parkland garden surrounding "The Argoed" (see the Millstone Country walk in this book). Leave this to curve left, instead continuing ahead to pass behind the old coach-house and the chapel, then through a kissing gate and across the lawns behind the main house itself. Go through the black-painted kissing gate just beyond the old driveway and flower urns and walk across the rough pasture towards the small greenhouse near the bungalow. Bear right just before this to find the slab-stile in the wall and once over this turn left.

Follow this winding back road (ignore the one immediately opposite) for a quarter mile or so, bearing right at the first junction, just past the "G.R." postbox, then in about one hundred yards bear left (virtually straight ahead) along the "No Through Road." As this surfaced road ends at a wooded clearing, go straight ahead along the main woodland path, downhill beneath a yew tree. Stick with this sunken track to reach a forestry road a few hundred yards away and turn left along this.

This gradually continues to lose altitude, eventually curving left around a sharp hair-pin bend. Don't go round this, instead take the narrow path which goes ahead-right from the start of the curve, a path which quickly steepens, cutting a deep gash into the hillside. Here and there the odd bit of masonry supports these steep sides, evidence that this is a centuries old pathway from the plateau down to one of the Wye's tributaries.

The sound of this tributary gushing along its bed heralds the end of this woodland path; bear right, then left to gain the minor road which sneaks along the bottom of this, the valley of the White Brook. Turn left down the road, within yards you'll reach the tiny Holy Trinity Church at Whitebrook. This dates from about 1840, its internal decor and features

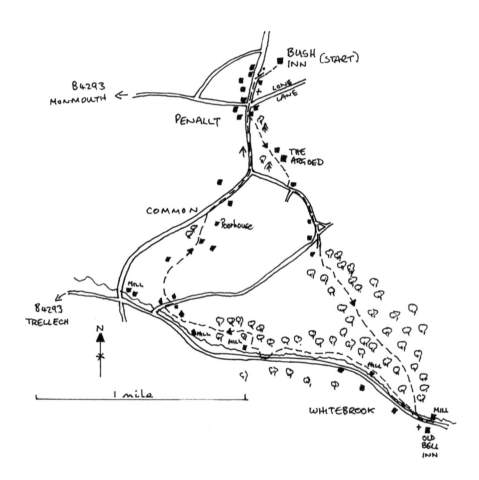

owe a lot to the Reverend Josuah Stansfield, curate at the turn of this century, who carved the intricate oak Rood Screen. Strangely there are no gravestones, slabs or memorials at this place of worship. It's said locally around here that George Bernard Shaw and Bertrand Russell, both staying at "The Argoed", came to grief after riding their bicycles "hands-off" all the way from Penallt along the backroads; they were charged by the local constable (who happened to appear on the scene) with being drunk and disorderly and later appeared at Monmoth Magistrates Court.

The old Bell Inn and Chapel, Whitebrook.

The large white house a few yards down the lane was once The Bell Inn, de-licensed now for many years but still retaining its last licensees name in the quarterlight above the door. A little further down again, this time on the left, is a considerable house on the valley floor adjoined by a series of ruins. These are just some of the remains of the thriving paper industry which once existed in this valley.

There were eventually four mills in the valley, the first dating from around 1760, established by a Bristol paper merchant, Henry Cotton. Large amounts of paper were produced, pack-horsed down to the Wye at the mouth of White Brook and shipped to Bristol. The quality of the paper was so fine that it was used for banknotes.

Old Paper Mill, Whitebrook

Strangely, the coming of the railway seems to have been the death knell for the industry. This decimated the shipping fleet on the Wye and the transport rates charged by the railway company for the paper were extortionate. Plans to build a branch line up the valley of White Brook came to naught and the last mill closed in 1888, leaving them to fall into picturesque ruin.

The mill near the Bell Inn was Clearwater Mill, further downstream was Wye Valley Mill whilst higher up the valley were Fernside and Sunnyside Mills. Substantial remains exist at most of the sites, although they're all private, the mill owners houses having been adapted as exclusive country residences. The valley is criss-crossed by footpaths and pack-routes associated with the works whilst in a couple of locations chimney stacks survive, once used to vent the furnaces needed to boil the caustic soda with which the paper pulp was bleached.

The valley saw industry before papermaking however, as early as 1567 a wireworks existed at a site below Clearwater Mill. There were also several grist (corn) mills towards the top end of the valley, at New Mills for example. Again, these are now all defunct, although a network of leats and ponds survive, some utilised until recently as a trout hatchery.

Return to the point above the church where you joined the narrow valley road and walk along the track (signposted as a bridleway to Monmouth) behind the cottages, walking upstream and staying with the gently ascending, wide path for about half a mile.

Down to your left, further substantial remains are now incorporated as part of a landscaped garden. Ignore the path down steps to your left (marked by a blue waymark arrow, the sign for a bridleway, but it would be a sure footed horse indeed which could tackle that flight of steps) and continue along the main path, keeping left at the yellow waymark arrow to eventually emerge on the valley road.

Turn right uphill, in a few yards go right again at the footpath signposted for Colonel's Park and Tregagle and walk across the dam, holding back one of the ponds which once served Sunnyside Papermill. This section of route is well waymarked, having recently been diverted.

Follow the waymarked path up above the pond and steeply up into the woodland until you reach three stone steps which climb up an old terrace. At the top of these steps ignore the three-way waymark post and turn left, walking along the top of the old terrace, lined with mature beech and oak trees. In late summer and autumn this is an excellent area to see many species of fungi, including the picturesque (but poisonous) red-spotted-capped Fly Agaric.

At the waymark keep left, remaining in the woodland edge well above the large red-roofed house to eventually reach a stile giving access to a long, narrow garden. Walk ahead along this and in front of the cottages.

The wide lawned area on your left here was once an old cornmill pond, the driveway you follow away from the cottages is parallelled by an overgrown leat. On reaching the narrow road at the end of the driveway turn right and walk uphill for about one hundred yards.

On your left, opposite the driveway to "The Hythe," a walled pathway leads beneath a bower of trees and below the foot of the cottage garden. Follow this path, go straight over the cross-field road (guarded by metal gates) and continue up this old greenway.

Continue on past the gable end of the white cottage; soon after this the derelict cottage in the rough pasture on your right was once the Parish Poor House. The track eventually joins the minor road which traverses the edge of Penallt Common. Bear right along this and follow it for about a mile back to Penallt, forking right at the war memorial to return to The Bush.

6. Millstone Country

Route: Lone Lane – Graig Wood – The Argoed – Penallt Old Church

Distance: 6.5 miles

Map: O.S. Outdoor Leisure Sheet 14, Wye Valley & Forest of Dean

Start: The Boat Inn, Penallt, Gwent G.R. SO 535097

Access: Although the pub is on the Welsh bank of the Wye, the easiest way to find it is from the English side. Find the old garage in Redbrook, beside the Wye three miles south of Monmouth. Virtually opposite this (just up the road towards the football pitch) is a small, rough car park. Park here and from the back of it follow the riverside path alongside the football pitch. Bear left off this, pass beneath the deck of the old railway bridge and cross the river on the footpath part of the bridge; you can see the Boat from the bridge.

Bus: Service 69 runs between Monmouth and Chepstow, Monday to Saturday approx. every two hours; alight at the Post Office in Redbrook.

A walk up the steep, wooded side of the Wye Gorge to the Penallt plateau, visiting an ancient church and many remains of the old millstone manufacturing industry. One short, steep climb, paths will be muddy after rain.

The Boat Inn (0600 712615)

This tremendous, tiny little free-house, nestling at the foot of a great wooded cliff beside the Wye, is by far the most enterprising in the region for its variety and choice of beers. Regular fare includes Marston's Pedigree, Wadworth's 6X and Theakston's brews, supplemented by at least four or five other beers. All are kept in the stillage behind the bar, all but quarried out of the hillside, and served by gravity.

The pub itself is just two rooms, quarry tile floored and warmed by a vast woodburning stove. A few old prints, photo's and notices decorate

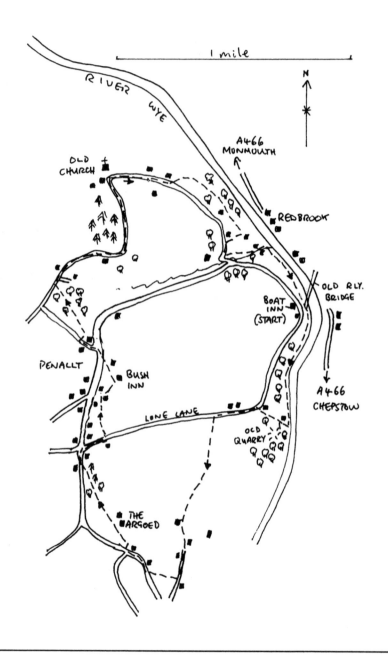

the walls, but there are no pretensions here. It's a fine old drinking den catering for huge numbers of walkers, fishermen, canoeists, mountain bikers and afficianadoes of the hop. It makes the most of its prime position with an adventurous beer garden created on several levels beside a stream which plunges over a series of falls past the pub.

The pub piano sees much use as The Boat acts as a venue for regular folk (Tuesdays) and jazz (Thursdays) evenings and frequent impromptu sessions by international rock stars, many of whom live in the area or work at major recording studio's in nearby Monmouth, most of whom also appreciate a decent pint or two.

The pub's name derives from the river traffic which once plied past on the Wye, a trade largely killed off by the arrival of the railway. The rusting old bridge, built in the 1870s (the footpath was added in the 1950s), once carried the Wye Valley Railway (later the Great Western Railway) across the Wye on its winding route between Monmouth and Chepstow, the line succumbed to Dr. Beeching's infamous axe in 1964.

There were stations at each end of the bridge, Penallt Halt at this end, Redbrook at the other, perhaps the two stations closest to each other on the whole British railway network. The Boat used to have its beer delivered by rail to Penallt Halt. Opening hours are 11 a.m. – 3 p.m. and 6 p.m. – 11 p.m.; excellent, even adventurous bar meals are available during most of these hours.

The Walk

Walk downstream from the Boat, beneath the railway bridge and follow the path through the riverside meadows. On the opposite bank a few old millstones litter the riverbank, on the near side the fishing jetties incorporate more of these implements. A few yards beyond the anglers' hut turn right at the waymark arrow and climb up to the old railway line. Walk up the steep, concreted driveway opposite and at the gateway turn left and climb the steep wooden steps/pathway outside the garden wall.

On reaching the wooden post at the top of these steps make a short detour to your left along the old overgrown track. This leads to one of the small old quarries where millstones were quarried and honed into shape. The whole site is now well overgrown, but here and there are scattered unfinished stones, roughly hewn into shape but awaiting dressing; one of these is pierced by a rusting old metal pole, as if ready to be mounted on a lathe for final shaping. One completed stone, covered in moss and lichens, stands upright against a fallen wall, still waiting to be collected.

The woodlands and common around Penallt are littered with remains of this unusual manufacturing industry. The millstones were worked from the native quartz conglomerate rock, known locally as "Puddingstone," in quarries on the plateau or delved into the steep valleyside. Penallt stones were especially favoured for use in cornmills and in cidermills. The major differences between the two seem to have been that cornmill stones were about nine inches thick and flat in profile whilst cidermill stones were twelve inches thick and convex.

Return to the wooden post, bear left up the edge of the large, overgrown garden to the white gate at the top and here turn left up the road. The garden houses a splendid, if somewhat overgrown, example of an old mule-powered cider press, the stone doubtless made in the nearby old quarry.

Beyond the slight kink in the road (c. 150 yards) go through the gap stile on the left and head across the pasture to the stile opposite. Once past the holly-filled hollow on your left aim for the far top-right of the long field, pass through the gate near here and cut the field corner to the slab stile beneath the coppiced hazels. The view has improved with each uphill step you've made. From this stile is an excellent panorama down the Wye to the wooded knoll of Pen-y-Fan, above Whitebrook and, beyond this, the great wooded amphitheatre below St. Briavels Common.

Once over the stile stick to the top of the rough pasture to reach an old trackway leading to and past an old barn. The rarely disturbed verges of this track support a great number of Greater Stitchwort and Mustard Garlic, a veritable snowfield of white blooms in spring and early summer. Continue along the track and through the yard of the house to a minor road, bearing right up this. In about 200 yards go right at the footpath sign and walk along the line of trees, some of them immense flowering cherries, up through the field, looking for the stile in the top hedgerow. Turn right along the minor road here and walk round the bend.

Just past the bungalow climb the slab stile and head towards the big house, "The Argoed." Go through the black kissing gate into the estate grounds and continue on line straight ahead. Cross straight over the minor driveway and walk behind the house, old chapel and outbuildings. The Argoed, dating mainly from the Sixteenth and Seventeenth Centuries, was once owned by Richard Potter, Chairman of the Great Western Railway. One of his daughters became, on her marriage, Beatrice Webb, wife to Sidney and one of the founders of the Fabians; their friend the playwright and critic George Bernard Shaw was a regular house guest at The Argoed, writing several of his best known works here.

The main drive away from the house is lined by a magnificent avenue of enormous trees, the various species used include some tall redwoods. Follow these redwoods, leaving the drive to bend away left, and cross the stile to reach the road. Go right, then right again down Lone Lane. In 200 yards, as the lane steepens, turn back-left along the old cartway and follow this round to Penallt's village green, complete with village pub, The Bush Inn.

Penallt is a Welsh name derived from two words, Pen, meaning head or edge and Allt meaning cliff or hillside. True to its name, the village is strung out along the very lip of the Wye Gorge, its houses and farms scattered around the village green, dispersed on wooded promontories or alongside the swift-flowing streams which cascade from the heights of Trellech Plateau to the Wye hundreds of feet below.

Walk along the old green lane away from the village green, The Bush down to your right. At the right-hand bend near the isolated cottage, also marked by a fir tree, climb the slab stile beside the gate on your left and follow the hedge to a further stile. Bear right down the road and then go left at the triangular junction, heading for Monmouth.

In 100 yards or so go over the new stile on your right and follow this diverted footpath around two edges of the field, the waymark arrows leading you to a wooded corner. Follow the obvious path down through these woods, parallelling a long abandoned and overgrown walled trackway, eventually emerging on a minor road. Go right here, ignore the side road almost immediately on the right and follow the "main" road through the dip and around the foot of the wooded Church Hill Common to reach The Old Church. In a few places are mossy wayside stones christened Pack (or Pecket) Stones, on these porters and carriers once rested their loads on the steep ascent from the ferry across the river.

The village's oldest surviving building, Penallt Old Church clings to the steep hillside high above the Wye, its Thirteenth Century tower anchoring it firmly amidst tumbling old gravestones in the steep, walled churchyard. Within the church several old memorials survived the seemingly inevitable attentions of Victorian restorers; one is of a local who died at Port Royal, Jamaica, a notorious city and refuge of pirates, including the infamous Captain Morgan. Rather obscurely, the Church stands on an old pilgrimage route to Santiago de Compostella, far off in the mountains of Gallicia in the Northwest of Spain.

Penallt Old Church and Lychgate

Near the lychgate a gnarled old chestnut tree marks the start of an ancient routeway down to the Wye; bear left down along the minor road. Immediately past the drive to Hillside Farm go left down the walled pathway and follow this, then the rough roadway, known locally as Washing Lane, past a few cottages and back round to the minor road. Turn left, shortly passing Birchtree Well, one of a large number of wells which once served the villagers.

Pause on reaching the "No Through Road" on your left and look up to the right. Here a walled trackway plunges down from the heights of the plateau above. It is paved with smoothed stones, polished over the centuries by countless millstones being conveyed from workings on the plateau to the Wye.

The finished stones were let down to the river Wye on ropeways, slipways or cartways, thence loaded onto coastal trading vessels known as Trows for distribution around the West Country and Wales, or even abroad as ballast in larger ships from Bristol and Chepstow. Many thousand stones were manufactured over several centuries, the last ones around a century ago. Some didn't make it much beyond the lip of the quarries from which they were hewn, the banks of the Wye host many-a-millstone which fell off a trow or was dropped into the river whilst being loaded.

The "No Through Road" is itself a continuation of this old millstone tradeway; follow this down, passing between several cottages to reach the riverside. Several of these saw service last century as cider-houses, one was even a pub, The Wheatsheaf. The steep track emerges beside the Wye at the site of the former ferry, a rusting pulley on a wooden pole the only reminder of this old river crossing. Turn right and walk downstream back to The Boat.

Old millstone trade route, Penallt.

7. Cwmcarfan

Route: Trellech – Cwmcarfan – Craig-y-Dorth – Gocket – Glanau

Distance: 7 miles

Map: Pathfinder Sheet 1111

Start: The Lion Inn, Trellech

Access: Trellech is about six miles south of Monmouth on the B4293 road to Devauden and Chepstow

Stunning views across South Wales are the main reward on this walk into and out of one of the great wooded embayments cut into the western edge of Dean's plateau, a walk mostly on back lanes, field and woodland paths with one long, moderate climb

The Lion Inn (0600 860322)

The earliest known reference to The Lion is in 1610 found, obscurely, by an expatriate Trellechian in a document in a library in Canada. Since that time, changes to the structure have been only minor, a small extension in 1815 saw a couple of additional rooms and the installation of a brewhouse (now defunct) in the cellar. For many years the pub belonged to the Cheltenham and Hereford Brewery, hence the "castle" plaque outside the door. Like many village locals it was left to run down, only to be rescued from closure in 1970 when it saw rebirth as a Free House.

The two public rooms could hardly be more contrasting. The lounge is essentially a cosy restaurant, comfortably furnished and carpeted, definitely not the sort of place to slump in after a long, wet, muddy ramble. It has an excellent reputation for food (particularly sea food) and features in many leading guides. The bar on the other hand is everything you'd expect from a village local – bench and wall seats facing an open fireplace, an uncarpeted floor and a variety of bar games including table skittles, an increasingly rare and much underrated game. Ramblers sampling the improving public footpath network in the area are made particularly welcome.

The beers on offer are Hook Norton Bitter and Draught Bass with occasional guests – Mitchells, Banks's and Wadworth's 6X for example. Opening hours are: weekdays 12 noon-2 p.m. (except Mondays) and 6 p.m.-11 p.m., Saturdays 12 noon-3 p.m. and 6 p.m.-11 p.m., standard Sunday hours. Bar meals are available at lunchtime, restaurant menu only during the evenings.

Trellech

Trellech (variously Trelech, Trelleck or Treleck) takes its name from the three standing stones (lech being one of several words in the Welsh language for stone) known as Harold's Stones, immediately south of the village. They've been dated to the Mesolithic Period (Old Stone Age, about 9000 years ago) by some commentators, the Neolithic Period (New Stone Age, about 4000 years ago) by others. Whichever is correct no contemporary human knows their function or significance, guesses range from the remains of a large burial mound to direction indicators.

Trellech also has numerous other relics to excite the antiquarian. The street name "Roman Way" reflects the belief that a Roman Road followed this high ridgeway between Blestium (Monmouth) and Venta Silurium (Caerwent).

Just beyond the churchyard you can't help but notice the great mound – The Tump Terret – of an old Norman castle. Southeast of the village is St. Anne's Well – "The Virtuous Well" – which for centuries was a popular place of pilgrimage, the waters said to cure umpteen ailments and even make wishes come true. It's said that an underground passage runs to here from Tintern Abbey, used by Nuns to partake in secret bathing rituals; maybe this was a fond wish uttered by a Monk of Tintern, as an Abbey was hardly the place to find nuns ..... A little way southwest of the village the woods hide the remains of Penarth Furnace and ironworkings, apart from those at Coed Ithel, near Brockweir, the only one known west of the Wye.

Completing the scene are old crosses in the churchyard (an Eighth Century preaching cross) and at Trellech Cross, a mile or so to the south; here also are the low, weather and farming-worn remnants of a Neolithic settlement.

Today's village is but a shadow of the settlement that in ages past was one of the largest Boroughs in Wales, covering 568 acres. This shrank to very little in 1291 when it was rased to the ground, and the inhabitants put to the sword, by a vengeful Duke of Norfolk, sorely miffed at poachers from the Borough who practiced their trade on his Estate at Piercefield, near Chepstow. A century later it was recorded that the town contained 86 uninhabited properties, a quarter of the total.

It recovered sufficiently, however, to hold a market charter and appoint a mayor, both of which functions survived until 1695. The size of St. Nicholas's church, out of all proportion to the current settlement, is further proof of the past importance of this now quiet village. This dates from the Fourteenth Century, but on a much older site – beside the cross in the churchyard is a Celtic slab-altar, complete with weathered carvings.

The Walk

Walk ahead from The Lion, the church on your left. Follow the road sharply round to the right around the Post Office and continue along to the small estate on your left. Turn left along Roman Way and walk to its end to find the small block of flats, Roman Court. Go along the paved path which runs immediately left of the flats and, within yards, climb the stile and follow the direction of the footpath sign for Cwmcarfan.

At the far side of the pasture locate the stile, beneath a massive ash tree and beyond the brook, and once over such walk up the field to Redbank Farm. Climb one of the gates in the corner here and walk ahead about twenty yards, then bear right between the barns and through the farmyard. Pass through the gate beside the corrugated iron barn at the far end and turn left up the field, following the line of fence virtually to the top corner.

Some twenty or so yards before the corner climb the gate on your left and bear right, walking along the outside edge of the woods, a youngish plantation of firs bordered by older oaks, thorns and cherries. At the far end go through the wide footpath gate and force a way through the few yards of undergrowth to reach a forestry road.

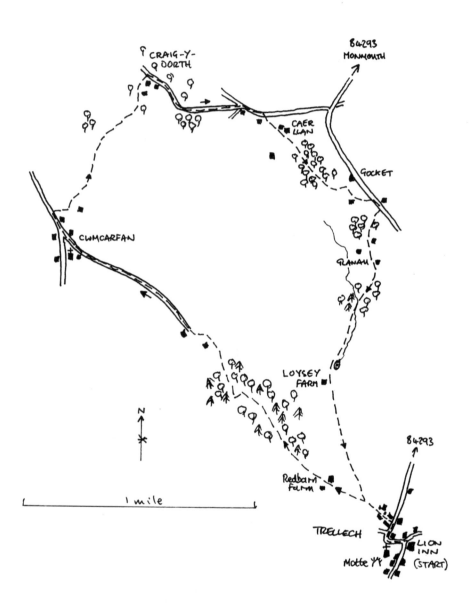

Continue ahead-left along this wide, sandy forestry road which bends sharply left in about 150 yards. As you round this bend look on the right for an old wooden field gate. Ignore this, but about ten yards below it an indistinct waymark arrow on a post points into the woods. Plunge into the trees at this point, picking up the obvious path which issues via a stile into a large, steep pasture. The next target is just to the right of the white-painted house nestling at the foot of the slope, so head for this.

This steep slope marks the edge of the Dean plateau, the point where the brownstones sweep down beneath the Vale of Gwent. This great bite out of the plateau's edge, honed by countless streams over thousands of years, is a great wooded amphitheatre blessed with endless vistas across Gwent to the Black Mountains and Brecon Beacons. Nearer at hand, the weathered ridge crest below is capped by a solid old church tower, this is our next destination.

Above and to the right of the house at the slope foot is a stile, a few yards to the right of the fenced-in spring. Climb this and descend to the old gate in the bottom left corner of the pasture, then turn right along the driveway. Pass through the works yard a short distance later and continue along the by-now surfaced lane for about one mile to arrive at Cwmcarfan church.

St. Catwgs Church, dating largely from the 1300s is one of a considerable number of venerable old churches dotted around this part of Gwent, most of which have never served a particular village but were provided by the local Lords of the Manors to cater for the needs of the scattered local community which has long characterised this area.

Many are renowned for the woodworking they contain, either in the structure or as rood screens, pews and suchlike. St Catwgs has a splendid barrel roof constructed largely from massive oaks; sadly the church is often locked but you can see in the eaves of the porch an old coffin bier on which coffins would be carried, or pulled by a pony or oxen, over many miles. Over the centuries these routes became known as coffin roads, and many-a rural church lies at the hub of a network of these, Cwmcarfan being no exception. Strangely, the graveyard here has more than its fair share of grand tombs and memorials.

From the junction by the lychgate head along the lane signposted for Raglan and Monmouth. Once past the barns go right, down the steep

Lane at Cwmcarfan

lane and bear slightly left at the fork, following the rough track down across the stream and into the field beyond, then commencing a long climb up out of the valley of Cwmcarfan Brook.

Climb a couple of waymarked stiles and you'll find yourself funnelled up into a very large, fairly steep field. The way out is half way across the top end where a stile leads into a very overgrown area of patchy woodland. Looking back from this stile, the far horizon is formed by the great wall of the Blorenge, west of Abergavenny and marking the eastern end of the former coal-mining valleys of South Wales.

Work your way up through the trees, heading for the top left corner of the inclosures, here turning right along the old cart track which winds up past Craig-y-Dorth Cottage. On reaching the narrow road turn right. This wooded ridge of Craig-y-Dorth was, in July 1404, the site of a battle between Henry IVth's troops, captained by Prince Harry (later Henry V) and Owain Glyndwr, scourge of the Marches and champion of the Welsh independence movement. Glyndwr won the day here, routing the English troops who retreated to Monmouth; scant months later Henry took his revenge at the Battle of Grosmont, harrying the Welsh all the way to their strongholds in the Cambrian Mountains.

Follow the undulating lane around the side of the ridge, selective views opening out over Monmouth to the distant Radnor Forest and westwards to the top end of the Black Mountains. Continue straight ahead at the junction and walk ahead to the telephone box near the lodgehouse.

Here go right, along the driveway signposted for The Gocket. This treelined driveway leads to Caer Llan, a large country residence converted from a school to a field studies centre in the 1960s. One feature you'll easily miss is a range of underground classrooms, built into the hillside by the ecologically-minded Director of the centre and which has received wide acclaim both nationally and internationally.

The public footpath passes in front of the house (either along or below the terrace, I couldn't find a waymark arrow) and continues to the sharp, narrow corner of the formal gardens a short distance beyond. Here, climb the metal fence and take the path which goes almost immediately off to the right. Within a few yards favour the left fork (i.e. don't follow the path along the edge of the woods) and follow this roughly along the contour. The path gently gains a little height before emerging from the trees at another metal fence.

Climb this and follow the wall on your right, climb the gate and walk above the old stone farmhouse to a rough drive. Turn left up this to reach the main road. The Gocket, to which the earlier sign pointed, is an old pub about 200 yards along the road to your left, it's now more of a restaurant than a country pub.

Turn right along the road and, within yards, right again along the road with its welcoming "Private Road" sign. It is, however, a bridleway, so continue along it, ignoring the various forks to the right which give access to the substantial estate surrounding High Glanau Manor. Continue on past the lone cottage and, a little way beyond this, along the grassy track in front of the sizeable Glanau Cottages, falling gradually down back towards the woods.

The second gate you reach is graced by a small Forestry Commission sign. Go through the footpath gate next to this and then bear ahead-left along the upper, level, path away from these gates. In about one hundred yards bear right along the forestry road which winds gently downhill and over the stream which has cut the little valley, all but hidden beneath massive growths of Great Hairy Willowherb and Himalayan Balsam.

Immediately over the stream, turn left off the forestry road and follow the water upstream. Climb the new stile, turn right to pass around the old, breached "dam" and then continue upstream over the stile and with the waymarks.

You'll soon reach a stile this end of a pond at Loysey Farm. Climb this and skirt the pond to the right, then bear left and go through the metal gate into the field a few yards to the left of the farmhouse. Bear half-right and aim for the wooded far-corner ahead. Here, a wide old wooden gate allows access to the woodland (n.b. there is currently [October 1992] work being undertaken in this area to erect new stiles, so the route between the farmhouse and this wooded corner may vary slightly by the time you read this).

Once in the woods follow the sometimes overgrown path through to the far side. Go straight across the forestry road and climb the new stile beside the metal field gate beyond. The next stile is virtually in line with the distant spire of Trellech church, once over which head for the field gate (and not the stile beside the wooden electricity pylon to your left), then pick a way across the marshy pasture beyond to the large ash tree at the far corner. From here simply reverse the first half-mile of the walk to return to The Lion Inn.

8. Cuckoo Wood

Route: Llandogo – Bigs Weir – Cuckoo Wood – Cleddon

Distance: 4 miles

Map: O.S. Outdoor Leisure Sheet 14, Wye Valley & Forest of Dean

Start: The Sloop Inn, Llandogo. G.R. SO 526042

Access: Llandogo is on the A466 about 7 miles south of Monmouth, The Sloop Inn is on the main road.

Bus: Monmouth to Chepstow service 69 runs approx. every two hours, Monday to Saturday, and stops outside The Sloop.

A long, gentle climb and a steep descent take this pleasant stroll from and back to Wyeside pastures bordering a village rooted to the gorge-side amidst woods and torrents. The walk is best done following a prolonged period of heavy rain.

The Sloop Inn (0594 530291)

This award winning Inn (Automobile Association Inn of the Year [Wales], 1985) is the sole survivor of dozens of pubs and cider houses which catered for the shipbuilders, crews, longshoremen and merchants of this once thriving river port. The name refers to a single masted vessel, more commonly called, on the Wye at least, a Trow. These shallow draughted ships plied their trade up and down the Wye, carrying largely timber, millstones and iron/wire/nails to Bristol docks; recalling those days, a large pub near Bristol's city centre quays on King Street is called the "Llandoger Trow", a mis-spelling of Llandogo.

The Sloop has seen many guises since those days of yore. It's currently split into two large rooms, a roadside public bar (with attendant games, juke box etc.) and a plusher lounge looking over beer garden and pastures to the steep wooded gorge-sides of the Wye. This was the original front of the building, securing most of its trade from the river rather than the road. A datestone suggests the Sloop was built in 1707.

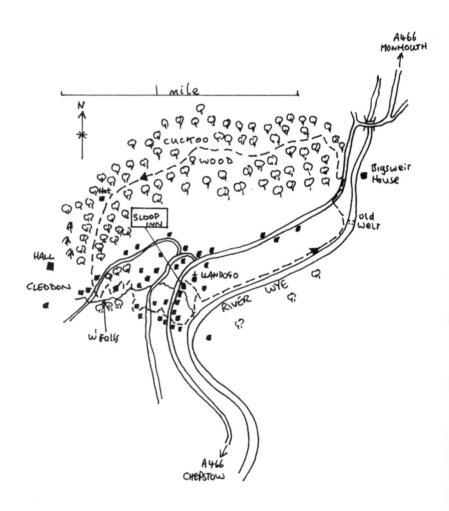

The beers on offer vary, but there are nearly always three available, usually including Smiles' from Bristol. As befits an Inn of the Year there are excellent bar meals on offer. The pub is open from 11 a.m. – 3 p.m. and 5 p.m. – 11 p.m.; all day Fridays and Saturdays (at least during the summer); standard Sunday hours.

Virtually next door is the village church, dedicated to St. Oudoceus, son of a Breton nobleman and a sort of alternative St. Francis, being renowned for his way with animals; he later became an early Bishop of Llandaff. His story and background is calligraphed on a framed document hung in the public bar of The Sloop.

The present Nineteenth Century church may stand on the site of Oudoceus's original monastery. One of its "treasures" is the ship's bell from the "William & Mary", one of the last ships to be built in the village (in 1860) which eventually rotted away in 1925 on the riverbank near the church.

The Walk

A public footpath sign points down alongside the left of the pub (looked at from the main road), walk down this lane, bear right behind the pub then climb the stile on the left just a few paces later. Cross over the old railway here, the former site of Llandogo Halt (which railway hastened the death of river-borne traffic already sorely affected by the rapid rise of iron ships from the 1850s) and walk to the riverbank, thence turn left, upstream. If there were any remnants of old wharves or buildings here they've all been long washed away by floods and high tides (the Wye is tidal for a further mile or so above the village).

The path hugs the riverbank for about a mile. The Wye is the Wales/England border here. Pausing for a moment on a hot, steamy summer's day the far (Gloucestershire) bank, mud flats and tree roots exposed at low tide, creepers and ivy tumbling from the trees, rotting tree trunks covered in ferns and the air full of buzzing and chirruping insects, is redolent of a tropical mangrove swamp.

The footpath follows the line of the old towing path alongside the Wye; 150 years ago gangs of horses, men (known as bowhaulers) or both would move heavily laden ships up with the tide or against the current, soon coming across Bigs Weir. This controlled the river at the point where the series of small islands and gravel banks now stand in the stream.

There were never any true locks on the Wye navigation. Instead, the weirs were constructed with an integral "flash lock" over which, by controlling the flow of water and allowing a good head of it to "flash" (flow) across a low lip, ships could be hauled. The towpath company was wound up in 1855, since when all traces of the flash-locks have vanished and rapids taken the place of weirs. Bigsweir Bridge, about a quarter mile further upstream, marks the tidal limit of normal tides on the river. The large house on the opposite bank is Bigsweir House, dating from around 1720 but built on a much earlier foundation.

The path curves away from the riverside at the site of the old weir. Follow the direction indicated by the footpath sign, recross the old railway and walk up across the pasture to the main road. Turn right along the footpath and follow this for about 200 yards, looking on the left for a footpath sign to Pen y Fan pointing hopefully up into the woods. This marks the start of a narrow winding path up through the trees; within yards it bends sharply left, then gradually right, continuing gently uphill past rhododendrons, yews and holly bushes, marked here and there by red tags tied to branches.

Go straight across the first forestry road and continue up the obvious path to a second such road, here turn left and follow it uphill. In about 50 yards this road horseshoes right; don't follow it all the way round, instead walk ahead along the somewhat greener, narrower road off the curve of the horseshoe and carry on uphill, ignoring the track to the right a few yards later.

This is a long established old roadway, falling from the heights of Trellech Beacon and plateau down to the ancient river crossing at Bigs Weir and thence up the steep eastern side of the Wye Valley to the old Forest capital of St. Briavels.

Here and there are sections where stone setts are still visible beneath the grass and moss – where the side stream cuts across for example. This is Cuckoo Wood, that particular species being just one of many which add interest to this pleasant stroll up the long, gentle incline; listen out for various Woodpeckers and Buzzard and look out for Nuthatches, Tree Creepers and the difficult-to-miss Jay for example.

These oak woods are littered with mossy boulders, blocks of Quartz Conglomerate which have sheared off from the resistant outcrop of such which forms the steep top of slope in the trees well above you. The green road you're following eventually emerges at a junction of forestry roads beside an old, tumbledown woodman's hut and store.

Hidden in the woods a few hundred yards behind this is Cleddon Hall, birthplace of the philosopher and pacifist Bertrand Russell. Turn left at this junction of tracks, not along the forestry road but down along the waymarked Wye Valley Walk, a wide track which gradually falls through the woodland and down from this highest point on this particular walk.

In about a half mile the path reaches a group of cottages at the hamlet of Cleddon. There's a wide choice of roads and tracks here, you want the one which is signposted for Cleddon Shoots and Falls. Immediately a flight of steep steps takes you down alongside a series of waterfalls which have cut a gash into the gorge-side here.

These are the Shoots and Falls, a renowned attraction in early Victorian days when the gentility, taking the Wye Tour by boat from Ross to Chepstow, would disembark at the wharves in Llandogo and climb up the purpose-built trail that you are now on to view this natural wonder. It's said that a ghostly form dressed in the fine regalia of a Victorian lady is seen from time to time, endlessly walking up and down the trail.

The path (after an initial set of steps up) descends through a series of switchbacks some distance away from the tumbling stream, affording occasional views through the trees to the Wye and, on the skyline beyond, St. Briavels Church. The whole area is a Nature Reserve owned by the Gwent Wildlife Trust.

Forester's Hut, Cleddon.

Just after you reach the point where a garage is visible down below you, a side path leaves the main path to the right at one of the sharp-left corners, marked by a couple of boulders and a tree stump. This path takes you back to the defile cut by the stream and across it on slippery stepping stones/boulders. (If the stream is impassable due to adverse conditions simply return to the main path and follow it down to the village). Once across bear left and follow the path along the steep side of the valley, leaving the stream to lose some of its momentum in the silty remains of a small old millpond just visible far below down to your left.

This path leaves the woods beside a white garden gate, just after which a footpath sign directs you left towards the A466. Go down this path and straight across the surfaced lane at the end, continuing along the walled path as if heading straight for someone's kitchen window. As you reach this the path falls away left down a long set of steep steps. Go down these and into a web of back paths interlinking the dozens of old cottages and villas which are rooted to the steep hillside of this great embayment, carved by the Wye many thousands of years ago. Essentially at any choice of paths take the one which goes downhill.

Go straight over a further surfaced back lane to reach a weathered old footpath sign again pointing to the A 466. Here, ignore this direction (which would take you down further steps) and bear right along the level path, winding between cottages and gardens and, in a short distance, down some new concrete steps to the A466.

Carefully cross this busy road here and go down the steps and path beyond, soon emerging in the riverside pasture beside one of Llandogo's former pubs, The Old Ship. Walk upstream and once across the footbridge head back across the pasture and old railway to the church and Inn.

9. The Angiddy Valley

Route: Trellech Grange – Barbadoes Hill – Old Furnace – Tintern Cross

Distance: 4.5 miles

Map: O.S. Outdoor Leisure Sheet 14, Wye Valley & Forest of Dean

Start: The Fountain Inn, Trellech Grange. G.R. SO 503012

Access: Trellech Grange is about 3 miles west of Tintern. From Tintern turn up the minor road beside the Royal George Hotel, signposted for Llanishen. In two miles turn right across the small dam and follow the sign beyond for Llanishen. The pub is a further mile on the left. From Trellech take the middle road at the junction south of the village centre, towards Catbrook and Trellech Grange. In a half mile turn right (just round a sharp bend) at the sign for Parkhouse. Carry on past the Parkhouse Inn to find the Fountain about 1.5 miles further along.

Pleasant easy walking with a few gentle climbs in and around the historic Angiddy Valley near Tintern. Woodland, fields and back lanes.

The Fountain Inn (0291 689303)

It must have been a sad day for local drinkers when this, the last of Trellech Grange's six pubs, burned down one dark day back in 1964. Fortunately it quickly rose again from the ashes, in the process retaining as much of its 350 year old character as was possible. Still there are low, massive old beams, many inglenooks and corners and the huge fireplace warming one end of the building.

The pub dates from at least 1611, the date visible on one of the gables pictured on photographs taken of the pub after the fire. These photos and a restrained collection of local prints and paintings dot the walls of the essentially open plan interior, furnished with an array of old chairs, benches and tables.

Furnishing the one bar are handpumps dispensing a varying selection of ales, Theakston's Bitter is a regular and Wadworth's 6X another favourite. The pub is huddled on a corner beside a bend in the Angiddy Fach's deep little valley and the beer garden makes the most of this situation; there can be few places as pleasant in which to sip a pint or three in this quiet, little visited corner of old Monmouthshire.

The Fountain is open between 12 noon and 3 p.m., and 6 p.m. – 11 p.m., standard hours on Sundays. Bar meals are available through much of these hours, there's also an excellent restaurant.

The Walk

On the inside of the sharp bend opposite The Fountain is a small, corrugated-roofed stone barn. Climb the stile to the right of this and cross the pasture to the next stile at the far side. Already pleasant views have opened up down along the wooded valley of the Angiddy Fach (Little Angiddy) brook.

Cross directly over the farm road and take the stile opposite, aiming then for the stand of trees some yards to the left of the stone barn. An interesting feature of this old building is the brick doveloft built into the gable above the door, offering perhaps fifty nesting sites which, in days gone by, provided a valuable source of fresh meat for the farmer and his employees during the winter months.

Work your way through the rather boggy copse just beyond Wain-y-Parc Farm using the sleeper bridges in the wettest sections. Leave via the stile and turn left up along the edge of the trees to a further stile, once over which turn right. Follow the edge of the field right round to the top-right corner, enter the field across the top here via another stile and head half left to the wooded top edge, keeping a keen eye out for the stile into the woods here which is hidden beneath a small oak.

These woods are somewhat overgrown, head virtually straight ahead through them, slightly favouring your left hand. There's no obvious path but in about 200 yards you'll hit a well used path cutting across the top end of the slope and along the edge of the woods. Turn right and follow this through the recently felled area of firs to a forestry road.

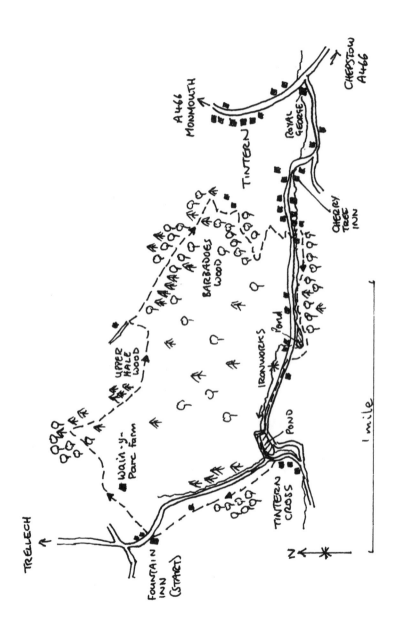

Turn right, then immediately left and follow the track alongside the woods, trees on your left. At the end of this stand of firs go left along the green path, soon cresting the top of Upper Hale Wood in the midst of a large cleared area. Down below the Wye remains hidden in its deep wooded gorge, parts of which you can pick out whilst beyond the declavity in the middle horizon the patchwork fields of the western side of the Cotswolds provide the distant horizon.

Bear left with the path and walk along through the plantation of Christmas trees to reach a clearing at a junction of forestry roads with the end of a tarmaced lane. Turn right here and stick with this wide Forestry road for about half a mile.

Yet another large cleared area has opened up views northeast across Dean to the distinctive hilltop of May Hill, west of Gloucester, crowned with an isolated clump of huge trees and a well known landmark from many miles around; the trees were planted to celebrate Victoria's Golden Jubilee in 1887. The great areas of scrubby felled and replanted woodland through which this walk passes are an ideal place to see (or more likely hear) Nightjars, 1992 was a particularly good summer for them.

Carry straight on at the fiveways junction of roadways then turn right at the next crossroads about a half-mile further on. Start round the right-hand bend and then go left at the fork and follow this narrower roadway downhill, keeping right at the next junctions and passing by to your left a small old stone barn. This track becomes steeper and much rougher, followed by a stream in the wettest of weathers. At the bottom the track issues into a complicated junction. You need to take the second left, the roadway which sweeps round the horseshoe and falls downhill. A short way down the hill go right at the "Tintern Trail" signboard which is at right-angles to the road and wind down through the trees to the minor road which follows the bottom of the Angiddy's valley.

Many of the old cottages which line the narrow valley floor here are contemporary with the Middle Wireworks, of which there are few remains, a little further downstream. Go straight across the road and up the lane which runs past Chapel Cottage. Just past the cupressor hedge on your right a footpath sign indicates the direction to Angiddy Ironworks. Go along this, up the steps and along the initially sunken pathway, soon developing into a wide, level greenway along a slight ledge in the woodlands above the valley floor. It's level enough to have been an old plateway or tramroad linking some of the valleys many industrial sites but records suggest use only as a path and pack horse route.

In around half a mile fork right down the steep path (marked half way down by a post) to reach a dam holding back an old millpond. This acted as a supply for the middle wireworks. Don't cross the dam, rather skirt the left side of the pond and cross a couple of footbridges, then follow the streamside path upstream to emerge on the valley road virtually opposite the ironworks (turn left up the road to reach them).

Old Ironworks, Angiddy Valley

These works have been dated to the early 1600s and are an integral part of a series of furnaces, forges and wireworks that once made this modest little valley one of the country's leading industrial complexes. It's generally accepted that it was the monks of Tintern Abbey who first developed the Angiddy Valley, creating what was certainly one of the very first wireworks in the world.

Lower Furnace Pond, Pontysaeson.

Their industrial foundations outlived their religious one by several centuries, the ironworks you are now at, for example, closed in 1828 as one of the last charcoal furnaces in the country whilst the lower wireworks (a short distance behind the Royal George in Tintern village) survived until this century, connected to the Great Western Railway via a tramroad and surviving graceful bridge over the Wye. The old turbine, powered by water, still survives in situ, buried beneath the wasteland.

The ironworks, Abbey Tintern Furnace, lay overgrown and all but forgotten until about twelve years ago when the site was comprehensively excavated. A series of interpretive boards outline the functions of the various buildings on the site and the method used to smelt the various ores which found their way to the works. The old blast furnace still has some of its old firebricks and even the yellow deposits caused by sulphur.

Return to the road and turn right, following it uphill for about a third of a mile to reach the dam at Pontysaeson; turn right onto this. The pond here is one of two which helped power the Upper Ironworks, the tumbled remains of which litter the woods up to your left. An adjacent forge provided the osmond iron which then was drawn through rollers and slitting mills to the required thickness for making wire or nails. The upper pond is now dry but the substantial dam survives.

Cross the lower dam and follow the road above the water to the junction. Here turn left and walk for about 75 yards to the first cottage on the right, Lilac Cottage, one of Trellech Grange's lost pubs. Immediately before this, and also on the right, a stile (replacing the official footpath nearer the junction) beside a field gate gives access to an old field road, doubling as a bridleway. Follow this uphill, soon joining the line of a hedge on your left. Pass by the pheasant pens, climb the gate and walk up to the old barn. Join the initially overgrown old track which runs to the left of this building and which, in about a quarter of a mile, brings you back to The Fountain Inn.

10. Lord's Wood

Route: Lord's Wood – Symonds Yat West – Great Doward

Distance: 5 miles

Map: O.S. Outdoor Leisure Sheet 14, Wye Valley & Forest of Dean

Start: Forestry Commission Car Park, The Doward. G.R. SO 548157

Access: From the A40 dual carriageway at either the Ganarew or Symonds Yat West turns follow signs for Crocker's Ash, then pick up signs for The Biblins and "Heritage Centre" here at the minor junction by the telephone box. Follow this single-track road (ignore side roads) for about a mile to the hairpin bend where The Biblins is signposted ahead along a forestry roadway. Go down this and keep right at the junction to find the small car park signposted on your right, about 150 yards down the road.

A pleasant mix of mature woodland, spectacular river cliffs, prehistoric remnants and riverside paths. One long, very steep and tricky descent, one lengthy but gradual climb.

The Pubs

The two pubs on this walk are encountered in Symonds Yat, about half way around. **Ye Olde Ferrie Inn** (0600 890232) is a well known and popular old pub right on the riverside, one of the pedestrian-only ferries across the Wye leaves virtually from the front door and gave the pub its name.

The pub's origins lie in the Fifteenth Century, it was busy from early times servicing an important crossing point where the old towpath changed from this west bank to the east bank of the Wye. Beers on offer here include Courage Director's, John Smith's Bitter and Bass, there's a substantial terrace and beer garden in which to sup your pint, offering an excellent prospect down into the Wye Gorge.

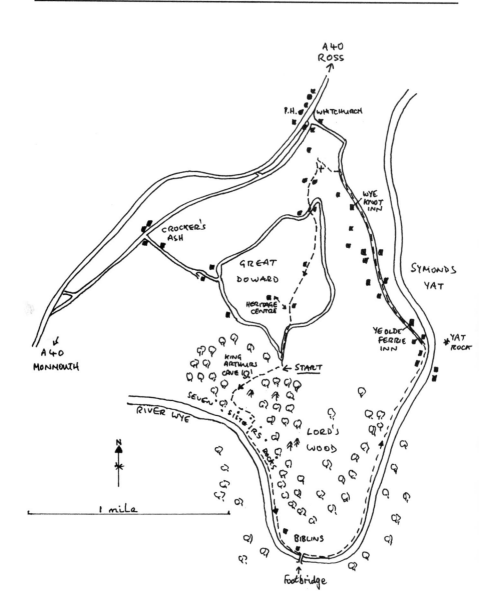

The other pub is **The Wye Knot** (0600 890501), a long, thin pub with a small bar virtually beside the entrance. It was originally The Grove Inn, closing in around 1969 only to rise again in its present form a decade later. Older locals still refer to the pub as the Jam Pots after a period during the First War when glasses and tankards were in short supply, so the regulars resorted to taking their beer and cider in jam pots.

No such danger today; the beer range may vary, on my last visit Wye Valley Bitter was on offer. There are pleasant views from the picture windows along the front of the pub across to Goodrich and Coppet Hill.

The Walk

From the lower end of the car park (a few yards to the right of the signboard) a wide path leads gently down into the fine mature deciduous woodland which characterises much of Lord's Wood. Bear right at the fork and follow the main path, gradually narrowing and falling down a few natural limestone steps. This path steepens slightly before reaching a clearing beneath massive beech trees.

On your right here are some caves worn into a small bluff of limestone. This is King Arthur's Cave, renowned in archaeological circles for the great variety of palaeolithic hand tools and bones of long extinct animals (sabre-toothed tiger, cave bear, rhinoceros, etc.) which have been found here during a series of digs carried out during the past century and more; Monmouth Museum has some of these finds on display.

Return to the path and continue in the direction in which you were walking, gently downhill away from the cave. The wide path gradually curves around to the left, glimpses through the trees on the right reveal Little Doward Hill.

In a third of a mile or so the path levels, ignore the path off to the right at this point and stay with the main path, climbing steeply up a series of natural steps in the limestone (to confirm your route there's a yellow arrow painted here).

King Arthur's Cave

Stick with this path for about a hundred yards or so, then go right along one of the narrower paths down through the trees. Walk carefully, for within yards the path reaches the top of one of the abutments of limestone which characterise this part of the Wye Gorge. Beyond is a long, steep drop down to the river several hundred feet below.

This rock is one of a series called the Seven Sisters which stand proud from the gorgeside and offer glorious views into the heart of the thickly wooded gorge. To your left you can pick out several more of the Sisters, to your right the others before the river sweeps left, out of this upper section of the famous gorge below the heights of Buckholt Hill. A breeze may bring with it traffic noise from the A40 a mile or so away, but on still days this is a serene, peaceful spot, occasional disembodied voices floating up from canoeists or salmon-fishers boating on the river far below. On the opposite bank of the river the course of the old railway, closed to passengers in 1959 and completely in 1964, can be traced whilst above the island, downstream, the old Hadnock Quarry, worked until the early 1970s, is rapidly returning to nature.

This is also a prime spot for birdwatchers, the mix of deciduous and conifers attracting myriad species – crossbill, hawfinch, all the wood-peckers, treecreepers, etc. – whilst the cliffs are home to kestrel, buzzard and peregrines. Lime-loving plants also make the most of these pinnacles, in summer look for the colourful red valerian growing on the ledges and the blue tufts of small scabious waving in the breeze.

Return to the main path and turn right. Only a short distance later you'll reach a crossing of paths, just beyond which the main path starts a climb through the trees. Ignore this, instead turn right and descend beneath the fir trees, soon arriving at a cross-path at the foot of these. Turn right and scramble down the path which here drops steeply down an outcrop of limestone, then turn left at its foot. The path levels out for a while, passing along the foot of a great cliff which, thousands of years ago, was undercut by the Wye, then just beginning to cut its gorge; the cavern-like embayments on your left are the result.

This is the point where a steep and tricky descent takes you to the riverside. The yew-woods are marked with myriad paths, all based on loose scree which makes progress somewhat hazardous. Simply take your time, select the option you're most comfortable with and scramble down the couple of hundred feet to the wide path at the bottom, turning left along this and walking upstream along the wooded riverbank. Stick with the riverside path as the trees peel back and walk along to the bridge at The Biblins. Take the chance to glance back from time to time to appreciate the Seven Sisters from this perspective.

The slender, wood and wiremesh footbridge was an early provision by the Forestry Commission of a recreational facility; you, however, should remain on this bank and continue upstream. These riverside meadows play host, particularly in summer, to large groups of organised youth camps and the area can be quite busy with these and with school field trips to the local authority study centre here.

Continuing upriver, various old adits, caves, rock-slides and natural clefts in the cliffs on your left provide interest. One of these hosts the "Dropping Wells" where calcium-carbonate rich water percolates from the heights above, depositing scale (rather like in a kettle) on moss, leaves and artefacts left by curious visitors, thus petrifying the articles – more or less an "instant" fossil.

On the far bank of the river a small stream gushes from the plateau above, this is the Whippington Brook, the course of which was once followed by a tramroad carrying iron ore and ochre from mines near Staunton to waiting boats on the Wye. The neighbouring little valley also hosted one of these short-lived rope-worked tramroads, conveying coal from Highmeadow Colliery down to boats and wagons on the main railway line. Adjoining cliffs are known as "The Slaughter", said to mark the site of a bloody battle between Saxons and Danes.

The riverside pastures fade away and the wide path once again becomes wooded. About a third of a mile past the gate out of the pastures, and as the main path starts to climb gradually, take the narrower, rather muddy path to the right which continues along just above the river. In the woodland on your left increasing occurrences of tumbled masonry become obvious, these are the remains of the once-substantial New Weir furnace and forges, one of the premier ones on the Wye; the weir itself was at or immediately above the island, the route of the leat leading to the bellows/blast can easily be seen. The island is an integral part of the famous Wye Rapids.

The path ends at a small white gate, go through this and along the enclosed path beyond, at the end of which go through the further gate, bear left up to the rough road and turn right along this. You'll soon reach the first of the foot-ferries across the Wye here at Symond's Yat, a sign directs you down to the jetty from where the rope-ferry runs to the few houses and hotels (and The Saracens Head pub) at Symonds Yat East. If you've a yen to take the very steep path up to the famous viewpoint of Yat Rock then take the ferry across and follow the waymarked route from the far bank.

Those who have worked up a thirst should continue along the rough road which runs along a virtual ledge above the river and below cottages, eventually emerging beside Ye Olde Ferrie Inn. A steep flight of steps leads down through the building to the slipway in front of the Inn, another chance of a cross-river trip or a break and a pint at this historic pub. The other pub in this, Symond's Yat West, is about half a mile further along the road, just follow it up from Ye Ferrie and walk ahead, eventually reaching The Wye Knot on your left.

Refreshed, continue along the road from The Wye Knot to the bend where a short stretch of dual carriageway has been created. Keep left, and from the outside of the curve an obvious footpath (behind a waiting restriction sign) ascends through the trees up a sunken pathway. At the top of this bear right along the minor road and walk along to the sharp left-hand bend. Leave the road here and go up the steps on the left, leading into the somewhat overgrown, small graveyard of the seemingly abandoned United Reformed Church; judging by the gravestones this dates from around 1800.

Walk up around the church and attached schoolroom to the top-back-left of the graveyard where there is access to a path climbing beneath trees and bushes. This soon emerges onto a driveway and, close by, the white entrance gate to a house called "The Cider Press." Just to the right of this a sunken pathway continues the uphill climb. The top and sides of this, Great Doward Hill, are criss-crossed by a complex web of these old sunken tracks, they were worn/constructed over the years by persons working at the numerous small quarries on the hill, and as routes to/from the centuries old ferries.

A steep, winding climb along this path ends on a surfaced road, turn right along this to reach the telephone box, opposite which go up the rough road, forking right just a few yards up this. Go straight across at the cross-paths then bear right at the fork by the tall hedge, continuing up beside the cottage and straight ahead at the cross-paths at the end of the garden. This path is a bit overgrown for the first few paces but soon becomes easier to pass, in a hundred yards or so emerging onto a rough lane. Walk ahead-left, continuing uphill and passing by the ruined little cottage to your left.

At the top go straight on, following this rough track to the junction beside the garage. The way lies left here, but along the drive to your right is the Wye Valley Heritage Centre, a remarkable collection of vintage agricultural machinery, ranging from threshing machines and early seed drills to tractors from the turn of the century. Here, too, is a vast collection of the forerunners of today's taken-for-granted household appliances – washers, sewing machines, irons and suchlike, collections amassed by the owners over several decades. It's open daily from 10 a.m.

Returning to the walk, follow the rough road away from the Heritage Centre, eventually meeting a minor road, along which bear right. The woodlands and old quarries hereabouts are part of the Leeping Stocks Nature Reserve, managed by the Herefordshire Nature Trust. Upon reaching the hairpin bend go left along the forestry road and right at the fork to return to the Forestry Commission Car Park.

11. Abenhall

Route: Mitcheldean – Plump Hill – Abenhall

Distance: 4 miles

Map: O.S. Outdoor Leisure Sheet 14, Wye Valley & Forest of Dean

Start: The Lamb Inn, Mitcheldean

Access: The Lamb Inn is beside the A4136, the main road through the north of the Forest between Monmouth and Huntley (& Gloucester)

Bus: Monday to Saturday service C24/25 runs hourly from Gloucester to Mitcheldean, two-hourly from Cinderford. Also a limited Sunday afternoon service.

A short, easy walk taking in two ancient ecclesiastical buildings and a renowned viewpoint. One moderate climb, some muddy paths.

The Lamb Inn (0594 542281)

The Lamb has recently undergone a major refurbishment, but one which has, unusually, retained a two room, two bar layout. When finally finished, this knocking about will have added a restaurant (with a distinctive and unusual wine list ... at least, that's what the vintner told me...) and generally tidied up this long standing roadhouse.

Formerly a Whitbread pub, now a free house, the final choice of draught beer was still being decided on at my last visit, one adventurous suggestion was Mitchells, from Lancaster.

The two handpumps are in the public bar, so don't despair if you don't spot any in the lounge area! There's a small beer garden at the front of the pub beside the rather busy main road. Opening hours are 12 noon-3 p.m. and 7 p.m. – 11 p.m.

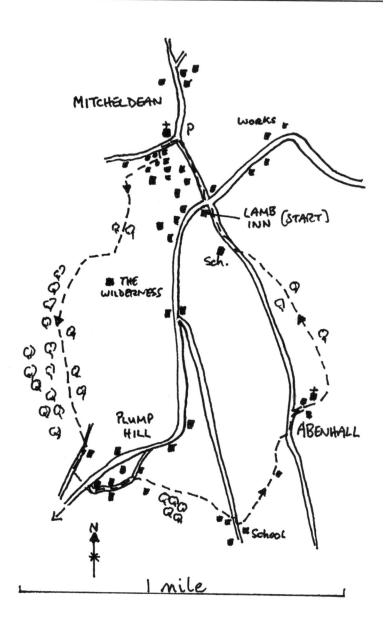

MITCHELDEAN

WORKS

P

LAMB
INN (START)

Sch.

THE
WILDERNESS

ABENHALL

PLUMP
HILL

School

N

1 mile

The Walk

Go along the road opposite The Lamb (Merrin Street) and walk to the crossroads beside the church, here turning left along Mill End. On your left here is a short row of medieval buildings, possibly a survival of a "butchers row" with overhanging first storeys; the house next to the black and white one was once the "Jovial Collier" pub.

On your right is Mitcheldean's pride and joy, the fine ancient church of St. Michael and All Angels, of late Norman foundation. Inside it's capacious and airy, with many wall-mounted memorials, including a double-brass one, the Baynham Brasses, dating from the 1500s.

To see the church's glory, however, cast your eyes heavenwards to the tympanum above the rood screen, upon which are some of the most spectacular medieval religious paintings in the country. The great barrel vaulted oak roof is also worthy of note, it, too, dating from the early Sixteenth Century.

To be frank, there's not much else to the town, a rather dour, forgotten sort of place with unkempt, derelict buildings, totally dominated by the massive Rank Xerox plant north of the centre. There are a fair number of old, even medieval, buildings in the town, but nothing is made of them, although Platts Row (opposite the library), a line of old cottages leading to the churchyard, is worth a look.

Continue along Mill End, which soon becomes Stenders Road, until you reach Baynham Road on the left, about 150 yards further along. Turn up this, then right a few yards later up the rough lane beside the bungalow. This narrows to a green trackway, at the end of which bear left at the footpath sign, climb the stile and follow the well worn path half-right up the hillside, beneath the cables and away from the modern housing development below. Glimpses through gaps in the ridge beyond the town allow views to Gloucester and the Cotswolds.

Continue up the steepish path through the bracken and brambles of this rough pasture to reach a short flight of steps and a kissing gate beneath the trees at the top of the field. Once in the field beyond this walk diagonally up the hill towards the point where the obvious estate wall at the top of the pasture dog-legs as it meets a wire fence. In this offset corner (n.b. not the narrow, funnel like corner at the end of the pasture) is a stile to climb, beyond which follow the line of wall on your left (surrounding The Wilderness, a majestic Queen Anne style house, once an isolation hospital now a field studies centre) to the top of the field. From this field are excellent views up to the range of the Malvern Hills, whilst near to hand the bare, rounded hilltop with the small crown of trees is May Hill, the trees planted to celebrate Victoria's Golden Jubilee in 1887.

Once over this stile follow the obvious path slightly left across the pasture to the woodland edge where a gate gives access to the wide track along the edge of the woods.

Turn left and follow this along the ridge, eventually emerging onto a surfaced minor road opposite a bungalow. Views to the right through gaps in the ridge-top trees stretch across nearby Drybrook to the top end of the Black Mountains, Hereford's boundary with Wales.

Turn right along the surfaced road, then go left at the crossroads, meeting the main A4136 opposite a stone house called "Bramble Cottage." This area is Plump Hill, once important as a quarrying and iron mining centre but these are now all long closed. It's also a renowned viewpoint across the sweeping meanders of the Severn Estuary to Gloucester and the Cotswolds, look through the gap in the ridge beyond Bramble Cottage.

Just to the right of this cottage is a narrow road called "The Rocks," go along this and fork left within yards, passing down behind Bramble Cottage. Continue downhill along this narrow lane to the complex junction just before the point where it starts to rise again back towards the main road.

Here, bear right immediately below the drive to Hillier Cottage and walk to the telegraph pole which also has a street-lamp attached to it. Walk along the narrow path which passes immediately right of this pole (i.e. not the rough drive to the cottage) and wind down this fairly well used right of way which snakes along the hillside some yards above the bracken-covered valley floor. Ignore any side paths and stick with the main route, here and there bounded by plum trees to the left and beechwoods on the right.

Abenhall Church

At the roughly-surfaced clearing take the track which goes ahead and downhill (rather than the one to the right up to a cottage), soon reaching a minor road. Turn right along this, then go over the stile on your left just before the small school. Climb the stile at the far side of the pasture and head slightly left, down into the shallow valley towards the small barn/stockpen.

Ignore the waymark by the gate in the valley bottom, instead head to the left of the barn and pick up the obvious, green, fieldside track up the hillside, keeping the hedge on your right. At the top turn left along the minor road, at the bend 100 yards further on go ahead along Church Lane (the "No Through Road").

This is the settlement of Abenhall, no more than a few farms, cottages and the little sandstone church of St. Michael. This was originally a Chapel of Ease used by pilgrims visiting a nearby holy well, the current building grew in stages between about 1300 and 1450.

It has some interesting old stained glass and a Sixteenth Century brass, but its treasure is the font. This dates from the 1400s, the panels of its octagonal bowl decorated not only with the coats of arms of powerful families of the day, the Warwicks and the Buckinghams, but also with the arms and emblems of the guild of smiths (tongs) and the freeminers (picks and shovels). Dues paid by members of these guilds, both strongly represented locally, would have helped pay for the building, isolated in now peaceful pastures beneath quiet woodland but which, five centuries ago, would have echoed to the sounds of forges and furnaces, iron-miners, pack animals and charcoal burners.

One suggested route for the so-called Roman "Dean Road" passes through Abenhall, maybe that traced by the bridleway the walk now follows. Walk along the road past the church and bear left at the bridleway sign.

Follow the initially overgrown track to the left of the field gate, it soon comes into its own as an ancient sunken trackway between high banks crowned with holly, elder and other species. Follow this to its end at Folly Farm and walk ahead down the road (or the separate footway on the left) back to Mitcheldean, meeting the main road beside The Lamb.

12. Flaxley

Route: Pope's Hill – Flaxley – Welshbury Wood

Distance: 4 miles

Map: O.S. Outdoor Leisure Sheet 14, Wye Valley & Forest of Dean

Start: The Greyhound Inn, Pope's Hill. G.R. SO 686142

Access: Pope's Hill is a scattered community on the A4151 about 3 miles east of Cinderford. The pub is beside this main road, at the foot of the long, winding hill falling from Littledean towards the Severn.

Bus: Coleford to Gloucester service 31A operates hourly, Monday to Saturday, and passes the Greyhound

---

A short, easy walk offering extensive views over the Severn and the Cotswold Hills, passing an old abbey and ancient hill fort. One long, gentle climb.

The Greyhound (0452 760344)

A substantial low, beamed old pub with a good mix of locals and passing trade. At its heart the large, partially stone-clad bar supports handpumps dispensing Theakston's Best Bitter and XB.

The main room sports an unusual array of timepieces, recycled from old clocks and watches, dotting the walls as well as the "traditional" brasses and prints. Continuing the unusual theme is a selection of duelling swords.

There's a large separate room/conservatory frequented by pub-game participants and family groups, leading in turn to a pleasant beer garden bordered by a brook.

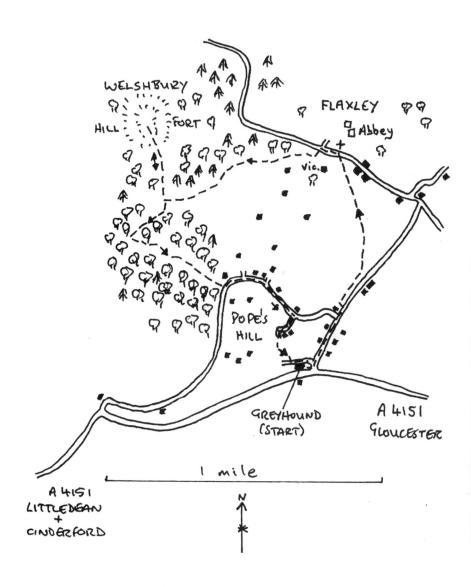

WELSHBURY
HILL
FORT
FLAXLEY
Abbey
Vic.
POPE'S
HILL
GREYHOUND
(START)
A 4151
GLOUCESTER
A 4151
LITTLEDEAN
+
CINDERFORD
1 mile
N

The Walk

Turn left up along the road beside the pub and signposted for Pope's Hill (i.e. not the lane behind the pub), winding uphill with this for about a quarter of a mile. Pass by the left-turn for Pope's Hill and walk on for about fifty yards, then go through the gate on the left, indicated by a public footpath sign. Stick roughly to the right-side of the field (parallelling the road), cross the obvious line of an old hedge and continue to the far side of the field, aiming for the stile a few yards to the right of the small willow trees. Once over this spare a few moments to take in the view, right, across to the Cotswolds. The tower of Gloucester Cathedral, its Cotswold stone perhaps gleaming in the evening sunshine, is just right of the line of sight to the farm silo in the middle distance.

From the stile walk along the slight ridge in the field to the gate at the far side. By now, St. Mary's Abbey at Flaxley has come into view, nestling in parkland below a shoulder of wooded hillside. It was founded in 1151 by Roger, Earl of Hereford for the Cistercian Order on the spot where, it is held, his father was killed whilst out hunting one Christmas Eve. Here and there are the few cottages and houses that constitute Flaxley, nowadays a peaceful scene but go back only 200 years and a forge and furnace stood barely 300 yards from the Abbey building, spewing out sulphurous fumes over the woodland.

From the gate aim slightly left for the spire of Flaxley Church, all but hidden behind trees and a slight rise. Climb the stile over the stream in the little valley and continue in line, over the snout of the rise and some yards to the right of the old manse (vicarage), bringing you to a minor road opposite St. Mary's Church.

The monks of Flaxley Abbey were, like their brother-clerics at Tintern, not slow to take full advantage of the natural resources Dean offered. By the early 1200s, King Henry II had granted to the Abbot of Flaxley the licence to coppice trees and use timber to fire the forges in which iron ore, locally won near Littledean, was smelted and worked by the Brothers and local peasants.

Flaxley Abbey

Such activity greatly added to the wealth of the Foundation, eventually to pass into the coffers of Henry VIII after the Abbey was dissolved in the 1530s. The first church, on the site of the current Victorian edifice of 1856, dates from that period. The Abbey and its lands eventually passed to the Boevey family in 1648, whose descendants still live there today; St. Mary's Church contains memorials to past family members. The splendid old Abbey building, a mix of the original structure and an Eighteenth Century rebuild, with attendant formal gardens and park-land, is easily viewed from the churchyard but is not open to the public.

Walk up the road from the church to the entrance to the Abbey's long driveway. Opposite this a flight of rough steps leads to a stile through the hedge, once over which climb another stile on your right and then walk up to and join the tractor road which curves up this pasture around the nose of the hill.

This narrows to a path beyond the hollow in the hillside. Views right from here are up the winding valley of Flaxley Brook, nowadays all but smothered by the endless rows of conifers. The valley once hosted three or four corn mills in this stretch, just out of sight one of these has been converted to a private house, retaining its millpond. About a mile up the valley are the scant remains of what was once a substantial ironworks at Gunns Mills. In this valley, too, the last known charcoal burner in Dean finally hung up his boots shortly after the Second War, ending a practice stretching back thousands of years.

Just past the hollow and attendant yew tree look slightly left to the corner of the woods ahead and walk to the field gate here. Climb the stile beside this and commence an easy ascent along the edge of an orchard of plum trees, the forestry plantation on your right. Climbing stiles as you get to them, a series of fields culminates in a very unkempt pasture, heavily infested with thistles.

Trace the path up along the edge of this field to crest the ridgetop at the line of a field road. Turn right and climb the stile beside the gate, then look left to sight a narrow, overgrown path climbing through the trees away from this angle between two forestry roads. This path takes you up to the substantial ditches and ramparts of Welshbury Hillfort, most easily seen during the winter months but impressive at any time of year.

Retrace your steps and recross the stile, then walk along the ridgetop field road and climb the gate at the far end, continuing along the forestry road beyond. The restricted views up to your right stretch to Plump Hill and the top end of Mitcheldean. At the junction of forestry roads turn left and then left again within about twenty yards, following this narrower, rougher roadway gradually uphill through the birch woods.

In about 200 yards bear left at the fork, passing over some black drain-inspection covers, the path immediately starting to descend. Pass by the fenced water company enclosure and continue downhill to reach a minor road, upon which turn left. This is the top end of Pope's Hill, from which are extensive views over the sweeping meanders of the Severn to the long line of the Cotswolds.

To your left (north) is May Hill with its crown of trees and, some distance to the right of this, glimpses of the tower and top storeys of the enormous mansion of Blaisdon Hall, now a Salesian School.

The impenetrable bracken cover of Pope's Hill Common hides a number of secrets. Excavations carried out in the 1960s revealed evidence of bloomeries (basic iron smelting sites) dating back to Roman times, amongst the oldest recorded in Dean.

Keep your eyes peeled and you may just see glimpses of a small vineyard well hidden behind the walls of bracken. Carry on downhill past the telephone box and turn along the first surfaced road on your right, opposite a white-painted bungalow called Delamere.

From this junction, the small Severnside town of Newnham is now in view, together with the southern ridge of the Cotswolds. Follow this surfaced lane until it peters out, at which point a stepped path leads down between hedges and fences to a minor road. Turn left along this to reach the Greyhound a short while later.

13. Lodgegrove Valley

Route: Vention – Lodgegrove Valley – Ruardean – Moorwood

Distance: 5.5 miles

Map: O.S. Outdoor Leisure Sheet 14, Wye Valley & Forest of Dean

Start: The Royal Spring Inn, Vention, near Ruardean. G.R. SO 604167

Access: The Royal Spring lies beside a steep narrow road just east of Lower Lydbrook and is well signposted from the B4234 Ross to Coleford road, up Vention Lane beside River View Cottage.

Bus: Service 46 links Cinderford with Lydbrook (and Ross) via Ruardean on Mondays to Saturdays. Service 35 runs between Coleford and Ross via Ruardean regularly on Saturdays, rarely on weekdays. In all cases pick up the walk at Ruardean church.

An easy walk along the course of an old tramroad above the Wye, then through a glorious wooded valley to virtually the highest point in Dean. One long, gentle climb.

The Royal Spring (0594 860492)

Hidden up a deep, wooded cleft of a valley, the buildings at Royal Spring saw a variety of uses before becoming a pub in 1832. No doubt the workers at the considerable bank of limekilns (recently partially restored) beside the pub stayed there. Before that the Duke of Monmouth used the building as a hunting lodge (hence the "Royal" in the pub's name) ..... maybe he even plotted his unsuccessful insurrection here.

One ageing resident finds it impossible to leave, the ghost of the last member of the Wheatstone family, the original licensees, still paces the upstairs corridors – maybe worrying about paying a bill from the local brewery which once supplied the pub and which now hangs on one of the pillars in the bar.

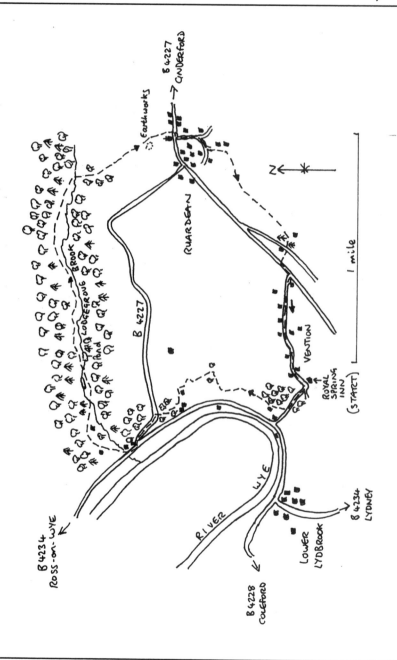

The "Spring" part of the name comes from the seven springs which still gush forth beneath the pub, adding to the flow of the tiny stream which has cut the steep, narrow valley into the edge of Dean's plateau. The owners have made the most of this setting, creating beer gardens to both front and rear, the latter also hosting a pet's corner to keep the kiddies amused, even quiet (the peacock and guinea fowl have raucous voices...).

Inside, both pub and bar are split level (the handpumps are hidden behind one of the massive supporting tresses, so don't panic when there appear to be none as you enter!), a mixture of bare stone and papered walls, myriad styles of table and chair all warmed in winter by a cheery solid fuel stove. A large adjoining room now acts as a restaurant, but famished ramblers can choose from an extensive range of bar meals.

Opening hours are 12 noon – 3 p.m. and 7 p.m. – 11 p.m., standard Sunday hours, last food orders one hour before closing time. The beers are well kept Wadworth's 6X and Worthington Best Bitter.

The Walk

Leave the pub and walk down the steep, narrow lane back towards the Wye. This was once the route of a short-lived tramroad, Scott's Tramroad, linking coal workings at Millway Moorwood, higher up the valley behind the pub, with wharves on the bank of the Wye; it operated only from around 1820-23.

In about 150 yards look on the right for a wide gate accessing a track which cuts away from the steep lane (there's a footpath sign here). Bear left along it and follow this level track around the hillside and beneath the woods, in a short distance passing behind (i.e. to the right) of the barns, all that remain of Watercross Farm. This track is the bed of another old tramroad, built in the early 1800s to carry iron ore and pig iron to small wharves on the Wye.

Beyond the barns continue along the obvious level, keeping the fence on your left. Down below the Wye meanders beneath steep, well wooded hills, on the hillside opposite the church and collection of buildings are at Courtfield, boyhood home to Henry V.

The Wye at Vention

Climb the gate half way along, then at the far end of the field (just past the rotting tree stump) turn uphill (ignore the stile in the corner) and follow the fence/hedge to the next corner. Here, climb the stile on your left then walk down the fields, keeping the fence on your right. At the bottom of the second field climb the gate beside the waymark (n.b. the second gate on your right) and then go left, following the rough lane behind the cottage and onto its driveway.

About five yards down this drive is a narrow path, obvious, if un-waymarked, leading steeply up into the trees on your right (if you reach the mossy old drive going off to the right you've gone too far along the main drive).

Walk up this to the grove of yew trees and, from here, bear half-right (n.b. not along the chasm but some yards beyond it) and follow this continuation of the old tramroad along the ledge through the wood. In a few hundred yards this emerges onto a minor road; turn left and follow this down to the Wye Valley road.

At the junction, walk ahead along the main road for about fifty yards to the driveway on the right, guarded by a substantial old lodge/ gatehouse. There's also a footpath symbol here, so walk up along this wide cindered driveway.

The large, flat area to your right is the site of the lower furnace in this, the Lodgegrove Valley. Today a seldom visited gash in the flank of Dean's plateau, it once resounded with the noises and echoes of a considerable industrial undertaking, first developed during the reign of Elizabeth I. A succession of forges and furnaces produced pig iron for use both locally and for export to the midlands by boat and/or tramroad (hence the level the walk has recently followed), only closing when technological changes rendered these works redundant in early Victorian times. The furnace closed in 1817, the forges lasting a few decades longer using pig iron imported along the tramroad.

A little further up the valley are more remains. To reach them, go up the driveway for about a third of a mile to the line of tall cupressus (marking the drive down to a house) on your right and walk up the left hand side of these (on your left a driveway curves up to 'Pink Cottage.'').

At the end pass the wooden barrier and bear right, initially downhill, along the forestry road. This is the route for the next mile or so, the roadway meandering along above the brook, bordered by great flushes of colourful tall flowers such as ragwort, willowherb, balsam and hemp-agrimony.

Staying with the main forestry road and gradually gaining height, this route first passes a rather silted up furnace pond on the left, the overgrown dam complete with a door giving access to its depths, followed a quarter mile later by a small, peaceful pond on the right which once powered the waterwheel of the top forge in the valley. This marks the top end of the old tramroad, its stone blocks and track lay rusting and unused for nearly thirty years after the abandonment of the forge before being lifted in 1874.

It's a considerable distance (nearly a mile) from this point to the next feature to look for, this being the point where the woods on your right, beyond the stream, give way to rough pastureland. This is the point to search for the path on the right (which can be difficult to spot in the head-high vegetation in summer) which drops the few yards to the by-now hardly noticeable brook, beyond which is a substantial stile.

Once over this walk ahead up the steep slope through the rather threadbare area of gnarled hazel and birch trees, slightly favouring your left hand. This soon brings you to a wall on your left, follow this uphill, climbing gates/stiles as necessary and heading for the steeple of Ruardean church on the hillside above. The fence eventually moves to your right side before a stile gives access to a grassy lane, along which bear right. The considerable grassy mounds and ditches on your right (and one solitary stretch of stone wall) have variously been described as the remains of a manor house and a motte and bailey castle.

The green lane winds up beside the graveyard to join the main street of Ruardean, turn right along this. St. John the Baptist's church dates from the Twelfth Century, its graceful flying-buttressed tower being added in the 1500s. Its treasure is in the porch, a tympanum decorated with a carving of St. George slaying the dragon, dating from the 1400s. The old heart of the village straggles along the main street and a few back lanes, infilling and considerable modern development have added nothing to this very workaday small town. Turn left up School Road, this side of the garage, and follow it round the bends to the fork, going right here then left up Kingsway Lane.

Climb steeply up to the hairpin bend and go straight ahead here along the bower between hedges. This old lane once gave access to mineworkings on your right, long since returned to agricultural use. Climb the metal gate at the end and continue ahead, hedge to your right.

Off to the left stretches the wooded plateau of Dean. You're virtually at its highest point here (a claim held by Ruardean Hill, at 951 feet, to your left) and this slight advantage allows views across the top end of Cinderford to the line of the Cotswolds, beyond the hidden Severn Estuary. Nearer to hand the sharp valley of Ware Slade cuts steeply down into the plateau, the occasional spoil heap the only evidence of the many small mines which flourished in this area.

Cross the stile on your right at the end of the taller section of hedge and turn left along the field edge, heading for the left of the Scots Pines visible in the middle distance and reached by several more stiles. The trees adjoin a road, turn left along it and look on your right almost immediately for a gate (at this end of the rough lane) into the pasture.

Walk slightly right, down this pasture to the gap in the rather tall,

Near Ruardean

gangly hedge and here pause to drink in the immense views. The long line of the Black Mountains marches across the horizon, their highest point is the tump about half way along, Waun Fach at 2660 feet.

To the left the Blorenge leads the eye towards the Bristol Channel. The gap between the Blorenge and the Black Mountains, guarded by the Skirrid and the Sugar Loaf, reveals views to Pen-y-Fan, highest mountain in South Wales (2906 feet). Further north, the expanse of the Radnor Forest rises beyond Herefordshire whilst the sharp hill in the distance, just as the view is lost behind the near horizon, is Clee Hill, highest point in Shropshire. In the foreground the Wye commences its wooded, looping course in and out of its famous gorge through Dean's plateau.

Continue downhill and slightly left to meet the bottom hedge about 30 yards from the right hand corner. Climb the gate beside the inaccessible stile here and turn left along the road, in about 150 yards turning right along the minor road for Moorwood.

Follow this increasingly steep lane down to return to The Royal Spring.

14. Bullo Pill

Route: Newnham – Bullo – Haie – Blaize Bailey

Distance: 6 miles

Map: O.S. Outdoor Leisure Sheet 14, Wye Valley & Forest of Dean

Start: Newnham

Access: Newnham is on the A48 between Lydney and Gloucester. Park in the riverside car park at the north end of the village.

Bus: Hourly service 73 between Gloucester, Lydney and Chepstow passes through Newnham, daily except Sundays.

An estuary-side stroll followed by a climb up onto the eastern edge of the Forest offering ample views over the Cotswolds. Some moderate climbs, one short, steep one.

The Pubs

There are three pubs in Newnham. My recommendation would be The Railway Inn on Station Road (the lane leading off the main street behind the clock tower).

It's a basic, unchanging local offering handpulled Bass. Several small, stone and tile floored rooms retain their small, cast iron/tiled fireplaces, the walls hung with various memorabilia including an old Rogers Brewery mirror. One room houses a very oddly shaped pool table. By the entrance door is an old Flowers Brewery, Stratford on Avon plaque, a brewery long closed.

The Railway is only open during the evening (from 6 p.m.). If you're in Newnham during the daytime, the other two pubs are The Victoria Hotel (open all day, opposite the church) and The Ship, on the higher side of the main street. Both sell real ales.

The Victoria is an old coaching inn (the old stables and coach house remain, partially given over to a garage) dating back at least four centuries. It retains fine panelling and a massive old staircase. There's also a curious, small windowpane on which is etched the old fable of the grasshopper and the ant. The original dates from 1622, the current one is a facsimile as the old one was stolen some years ago.

Newnham

There are two main roads to the village. Church Street, running close to the riverside, retains many old villas, cottages and the occasional barn/warehouse which recall the days when Newnham was a thriving port both importing and exporting iron ore and pig iron, exporting coal and wood products. It was also one end of a busy cross-estuary ferry, thought to be of pre-Roman origins and which last operated in 1948, the old slipway can still be seen at the end of Severn Street. An early competitor to this ferry was mooted in 1810 when Newnham was identified as one end of a planned Severn Tunnel but this, like many such plans, died a death.

The muddy expanses here at low tide now cover over what were once renowned sands, in the 1920s it was a favourite Sunday outing from Forest towns to take the local train or charabanc to Newnham and promenade along the sands or the "esplanade" up towards Broadoak. The many old pubs (look for the house names) help recall these high days.

Some buildings are built, at least partially, from very dark, shiny stone. This is dross from a major glassworks which once traded in the town, said to be the first in England to produce glass using coal as the heat source; it closed in about 1700. The old castle mound stands in private grounds opposite the church at the top end of the High Street. This is lined by a wonderful mix of grand Georgian houses, late-medieval cottages and Victorian infilling, the whole divided down the centre by a long, winding green which once sported back-to-back cottages, it's now dominated by the tall, slender clock tower.

The church has had a chequered career, the original one being lost to the shifting sands of the Severn (although the old font survives in today's building), a later one damaged by an explosion in the Civil War and a

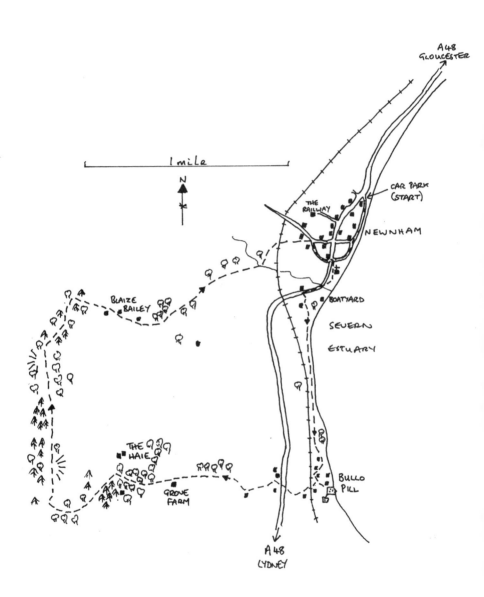

Victorian one burning down soon after construction. The current one includes a memorial window to the local Kerr family, a member of which married Sir Humphrey Davy, the inventor of the miners safety lamp.

The Walk

The walk starts from the churchyard of St. Peter's Church, at the south end of the village. To get here from the car park (marking the site of Newnham's once busy boat-building yards where vessels up to 600 tons were constructed) take either the narrow Church Street or the main road which meet outside the church.

Walk through the graveyard to the south end of the churchyard, from which are excellent views down the Severn as she sweeps around the great curves of Arlingham and Awre. On the opposite bank the isolated white building is a pub at the other end of the old ferry crossing of the river, now a popular meeting place for the hoards of birdwatchers for whom the estuary is such a draw. On this bank you get glimpses of several vessels moored at the still-extant boatyard.

The walk heads for this: go down the steep path from the churchyard and then alongside the busy main road for about one hundred yards to the signpost on the left for the Severn Way footpath (opposite the old farmhouse). Turn left into the driveway then bear right with the waymark arrow, following this green track towards the riverside. Off to your left is the old boatyard at Collow Pill.

Stay with the greenway, cross the stream and follow the tractor road through the meadow, the railway soon joining the route to your right. At the gate pause to look back, there's an excellent view to the church at Newnham on its river-cliff, the boatyard in the foreground and a vista upriver to Broadoak and the church spire at Westbury. Beyond the gate a rough tree-lined roadway traces a course beside the railway, at the end of the pasture beyond the trees cross the rough driveway/turning area and climb the stile beside the bungalow grandiosely named Kindlands Manor.

Follow the narrow path then gravelled roadway to the footpath sign just beyond the rubber factory and go left here along the Severn Way, straight across the surfaced road and along to the old dock at Bullo Pill.

This once thriving little port was initially developed in the early 1800s, connected by a tramroad to the ironworks at Soudley and Cinderford in 1809, part of the course of which was in a tunnel under Haie Hill, now claimed as the world's first railway tunnel. Initially, cargo was almost exclusively coal which was ferried across the Severn to the Thames & Severn and Stroudwater Canals for onward transport to the Cotswolds and beyond, or sent right down the Severn Estuary to the major docks at Bridgwater, in Somerset. As well as iron and coal the dock saw export of timber and bark and, obscurely, traffic in marble for a works which stood to the north of the dock. There was also a wagon building and repair works (now the rubber factory).

For a time Bullo was one of the busiest of the estuarine ports, steamships finding it easier to dock here than at Lydney. A branchline connected the port to the nearby main railway line. With the contraction of the iron, then coal industries, however, business ebbed away and with it the raison d'etre for the dock. The last recorded use was in 1926, soon after which the lock gates failed. All the buildings, cranes and hoppers are now gone, leaving the dock to silt up, useful now only to a few small cruisers which enter the mooring at high tide.

Retrace your steps to the surfaced road in front of "Severn View" house and turn left following this, the course of the old tramroad, beneath the main line and along to the main road.

Go virtually straight over this and along the rough lane beside the telephone box, near the forlorn but nonetheless impressive ruined building gradually loosing its fight against creepers and weeds. Simply stay with this lane, high hedged and in autumn festooned with blackberries and the bright red berries of Woody Nightshade (Bittersweet), which eventually passes through a gate and, by now surfaced, runs alongside woodland to Grove Farm.

Leave the lane to sweep into the yard, instead continuing ahead up beside the pantile-roofed barn. There should be a new bridleway gate here by the time you read this, pass through this and carry on up the sunken track to the woodland edge at the top of the field. This is an ancient track, recorded as "The Ridgeway" in documents dating from the 1200s.

Ahead-right you'll catch glimpses of the great old house, The Haie. This dates from around 1770, built near the site of a medieval lodge belonging to Gloucester Abbey. Owned by the locally-influential Jones family, then the Kerrs, it was split into flats just after the Second War. One of its treasures was a ceremonial sword said to have been presented to The Corporation of Newnham by King John, it's now kept for safekeeping in Gloucester Museum. The deep little valley to your right marks the course of the old tramroad, the blocked off tunnel starts at the woodland edge.

The walk continues up through the woods, go through the new gate and wind up with the path, going straight ahead at the junction of rough roadways and past the driveway to "Wenslark." Bear left in front of the ruined small barn and walk on a few yards. Before you reach the wooden gate across the road look on your left at the bend for a stile all but buried beneath an overgrowth of Knotweed.

Climb this and follow the woodland edge path gradually down into the valley, crossing stiles as necessary. Footprints suggest a head of deer in the woods here, largely fir trees growing on a series of ditches and hollows. It's no more than a fanciful, fleeting thought to associate these ditches with early medieval ones which will have surrounded the deer park here in Norman times, Haie being an old word for a deer park.

Where the fence on your right cuts away from you continue ahead across the rough muddy roadway and along the still obvious path to the few steps leading down to a junction of forestry roads. Here walk a few yards along the roadway towards the steep pasture ahead. As this bears right look for the wooden-rail "stile" on your left which gives access to the field, then walk up the steep edge of this field, trees to your right. At the top corner of the field a further stile leads to a grassy path, turn right along this to the forestry road and bear right up along this.

In a few hundred yards a lay-by has been created at a point taking full advantage of the stunning views to be had from this, Fernbrake Hill, across to the Cotswolds and over the great sweeps of the Severn. Some of the sharp, wooded edges of the Cotswolds stand out well including Nibley Knoll, capped by Tynedale's Tower, a Victorian folly built to commemorate the supposed birthplace of William Tynedale, translator of the Bible into English in the 1530s. Nearer to hand is the back of The Haie, its varied architectural styles and colour-washes bringing to mind Portmeirion.

About half a mile further up the roadway another lay-by, this time on the left, allows views across the heart of the Forest, nestling in its clearing in the winding valley below is Soudley, marking the western end of the old tramroad tunnel.

Follow the forestry road for a further hundred yards or so to reach, on your right, a green-waymarked post. Behind this, look for the yellow arrow painted on a tree, this marks the route to take and, once beneath the trees, an obvious, quite steep and muddy path develops. This falls beneath mature fir woods, home to crossbills but noticeably alive with goldcrests, Britain's second-smallest bird. Simply stand still for a short time and focus on the high-pitched twitter it emits every few seconds, you shouldn't have much difficulty in spotting the tiny bird flitting across the leafless lower branches of the spruces.

This path joins a forestry road at a clearing, walk ahead up the road for about one hundred yards then go right, along the rougher road which leaves the original road at right angles just before a left hand bend. Follow this straight across the junction, your route soon confirmed by a yellow waymark on a post to your left. The roadway emerges beside an old barn, one of several buildings here at the old Blaize Bailey Farm. Carry on along the path, eventually reaching the old farmhouse, the old water butt still full and ragged remains of curtains flapping behind broken windows. Continue past this to the well-roofed stone barn and pass to the right of this, past the "garage" beside the barn and down the field to the stile now visible beneath an ash tree.

Beyond this follow the path along the left of the field and across the back of the deep coombe cut into the hillside here. Turn left with the fence at the end of the woods on your left and climb the stile beside the field gate, then bear half-right, passing to the right of the isolated old ash down in another of the coombes in this area and aiming for the end of the band of woodland on the ridgetop ahead. Climb the stile here and turn left, descending gradually beside a fence and heading virtually directly towards a large, cream-painted house in the middle distance. Beyond this, views extend up the Vale of Severn and across to Gloucester, its cathedral tower easily visible.

Once over the stile at the foot of this field and carry on alongside this old apple and pear orchard for a hundred yards or so to a further stile in a short row of oaks. Climb this and walk through the threadbare orchard, cross the stream beneath the great old ivy-clad ash tree and then take the stile and plank-bridge on your right. Within a few yards a railway overbridge comes into view, cross this and follow the fieldside path beyond up to the copse on the hillock ahead.

At the end of the path beside these trees, climb the stile and turn right along The Green, once the village pound and pinfold, winding along which brings you back to Newnham's main street beside The Victoria Hotel.

15. Staunton's Stones

Route: Staunton – Kymin – Highmeadow Woods – Near Hearkening Rock

Distance: 7 miles

Map: O.S. Outdoor Leisure Sheet 14, Wye Valley & Forest of Dean

Start: The White Horse Inn, Staunton. G.R. SO 547126

Access: Staunton is on the A4136 road about 3 miles east of Monmouth.

A walk largely along forestry roads in probably the best area to see deer in the Forest. Also offers huge views from beside a unique naval memorial and visits some of Dean's most renowned natural monuments.

The White Horse (0594 33387)

The drinking area in this modest roadside house is deceptively small, just a small bar serving one moderately sized room; the other half of the public area is given over to a restaurant. The bar room is pleasantly, if simply furnished and decorated by a smattering of brasses, plates, the occasional piece of old yoke or harness and a few small animal traps, the whole warmed in winter by an open fire.

This, the last survivor of a number of alehouses in the village, offers well kept Flowers IPA and Boddingtons to the mixed clientele of locals and a regular trickle of ramblers in this rather off the beaten track village. There's a large beer garden and children's play area set off the pub's car park. Bar meals are available, the White Horse (one of a number dotted throughout the Marches which claims to be, geographically, the "First Pub in England") is open each day from 12 noon – 2.30 p.m. and 7 p.m. – 11 p.m. (10.30 Sundays).

Staunton itself has an old core of winding lanes lined with cottages and farms with a limited amount of infilling. To the south and east of the village are scattered remains of old iron ore and ochre workings, once linked to the Wye by the mysterious Whippington Tramroad, mysterious as there are no firm records as to its route. The village church is worthy of note as one of the oldest in Dean, a Norman construction (c. 1100 A.D.) based on an original Saxon site. It houses a font which may be a part of a Roman altar and an unusual stone pulpit reached from a spiral staircase which winds up into the recesses of the leaning churchtower.

The Walk

Go left from the pub and in about 50 yards left again up the surfaced road by the speed restriction sign. Almost immediately, on your right, is one of the lesser known of Staunton's stones christened, for obvious reasons, the Frog Stone or Frog's Mouth.

Follow the direction indicated by the yellow arrow painted on the gate just a few yards further up the road and bear right off the road, following the obvious, if bracken-plagued, path up alongside the wall and woodland, ending up some half-mile later at a triangulation column (trig. point) on this hilltop above Staunton. The concrete block beside the pillar is all that remains of an old fire watchtower that once stood at this commanding viewpoint, views that stretch well beyond the Forest into South Wales and across to the Cotswolds.

The main focus of interest here is the Buck Stone, immediately over the lip of the hilltop to the north of the trig. point. This large boulder of conglomerate was once a logan stone, that is one which was finely balanced on one point and could be caused to rock to-and-fro simply by gently pushing it. Some not-so-gentle Victorians (some say slightly under the weather after a prolonged sojourn in one of Staunton's pubs) forgot their own strength one summers day in 1885 and sent the rock plummeting from its pedestal. The reward for their endeavours was a bill for £500 from the local militia who tried in vain to rebalance the stone; since that day it has been firmly cemented in place.

The name Buck Stone is said to derive from an incident in the mists of time when the stone was an important Druidical site. On one particular feast day the Druids demanded a customary sacrifice, plumping for the

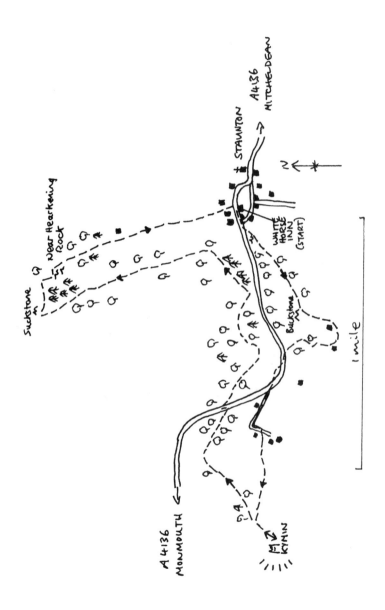

first living creature to come to the stone on that day. Not unexpectedly (for the sake of this story...) the first creature was a local youth, strangely unaware of this custom. Graciously accepting his fate, he awaited the fall of the druidical blade when, as chance would have it, a buck (male deer) fleeing from huntsmen broke from the trees and collapsed exhausted beside the stone. You can but imagine his surprise when he was immediately taken to be a sign from the gods as the true sacrifice and quickly dispatched, leaving the grateful local youth to grow up to become a renowned bard.

A few yards from the trig point a footpath signpost offers a choice of paths, favour the one for Redbrook and walk down through the bracken. Ahead, the splendid church tower and attendant cottages in the middle distance are at Newland. Pass by the tile-festooned house and bear right beyond it to reach the entrance gate to a County Council Adventure Centre.

Here, turn right your side of the gate and follow the initially wide track down back towards the trees. At the junction by the electricity pole bear right along the narrower path which soon brings you to a clearing in the trees. At the far end of this take the path off to the left beneath the large beech tree and follow this well defined path down just inside the trees to reach the main road at the bottom.

Cross this and bear left, cutting the corner via the large lay-by. Continue along the road for about 150 yards and then bear left along the narrow "No Through Road." Follow this uphill and round the sharp left-hand bend, ignore the footpath sign on the right and continue to the far end of the holly/cupressor hedge beyond the house on the right. Here is a stile on the right (and a homemade signpost on the left indicating the path to The Kymin and Naval Temple).

Walk up the field, heading for the left of the transmitter masts which are visible on the ridgetop. At the top of the field take the stile on the left and cross the manicured lawn to the white-painted round house here on top of The Kymin.

The top of this modest summit, barely 800 feet high, was an early purchase of The National Trust which body paid £300 for the site in 1902. The Round House was built around 1800 by "The Gentlemen of

Naval Temple, The Kymin.

Monmouth", essentially a dining club with a desire for a table with a view. They also constructed themselves a bowling green, still there although not currently exactly in a state of championship readiness.

A few yards below the summit is the unique Naval Temple, also completed in 1800, this time for the Duchess of Beaufort (hostess at Troy House, Monmouth's stately home) and dedicated to the glory and memory of those English admirals who ensured that Britannia continued to rule the waves. It's more than coincidence that the earliest such seafarer so-commemorated was Admiral Boscawen, the Duchesses' father. Nelson visited the Temple in 1802 – his name was already on one of the attached plaques – whilst on a tour of inspection of the timber reserves of the Forest, was said to be most touched by the project and joined The Gentlemen for a banquet at The Round House.

The Gentlemen's quest for a table with a view was most amply rewarded from their hilltop folly. Monmouth is spread out at your feet, Troy House is the great mansion down to your left. On a clear day the highest peaks of the Brecon Beacons are easily picked out, the Skirrid and Sugar Loaf seem near enough to touch despite being at the far side of the verdant Vale of Gwent.

Retrace your steps to the bottom corner of the lawn, climb the stile and follow the obvious path which cuts diagonally across this rough pasture. This field, and most of the others on the Kymin, are dotted with blocks and boulders of conglomerate; from this feature the hill takes its name, Kymin is a form of the Welsh "Cae Maen" meaning "stoney field". As the path gradually descends, views open out northwards to the line of the Malvern Hills, perhaps England's oldest hills. Pass through the area of trees and continue down to the stile at the foot of the pasture. Once over this turn right along the wide forestry road and follow this to its end.

Turn left and immediately cross the main road, looking for the stile giving access to a narrow path on your right. This falls through the trees to emerge on another forestry road. Turn right along this and remain with it, bearing right at the junction. This road is better surfaced than many you'll find in urban areas and offers pleasant, easy walking through the mature oak and beech woodlands here in Highmeadow Woods. This next couple of miles is the area you're most likely to see fallow deer without really trying. More often than not two or three will run across the road in front of you, or a crashing sound in the woodland gives away the location of a browsing animal disturbed by your passing – if you're quick enough you'll catch a glimpse. The verges are awash with wildflowers – willowherbs, woodspurge, dogs mercury, balsam and agrimony, bluebells, celandines and anemones all attract a wide variety of butterflies and moths.

The roadway gradually gains height before horse-shoeing right at a junction. Here bear left and walk down along the slightly rougher-surfaced forestry road. In a few hundred yards a great area to your left has been felled in recent years, this area seems a favourite one for buzzard to survey and hunt, there are nearly always at least two soaring above the steep, overgrown valleysides which take Forest streams steeply down towards the distant Wye.

In about a mile a yellow waymark arrow painted on a boulder points right, straight up at the Suckstone. This has the reputation of being the largest single block of stone in England, a massive lump of quartz conglomerate which has slumped from the sheer escarpment hidden in the woods above. It also has a certain reputation amongst collectors of semi-precious stones as there are many garnets contained within its bulk.

The name Suckstone is of uncertain derivation, what is certain is that it was originally attached to the pronounced escarpment a hundred or so feet higher up the slope (one suggestion is that this is the derivation of the name, the stone suckling at the mother-rock).

Follow the waymarked track to the right of the Suckstone and up through the dark shadows of the fir woods beyond. This path ends at the base of an undercut cliff of the conglomerate, Near Hearkening Rock. To find the top turn left along the base and wind with the path up around the side of the outcrop. The path needed to leave the Rock is the one which angles away from the edge at a tangent, traced by a waymark arrow. Before leaving, however, there are two or three suitable perches on the very edge of the escarpment which offer good views across this part of the Forest.

Follow the path away from the edge to reach a well used forestry road, turn right along this and follow it back to Staunton, reaching the village at the back end of a small new housing development virtually opposite The White Horse.

16. English Bicknor

Route: Joyford – English Bicknor – Mailscot Wood – Hillersland

Distance: 6.5 miles

Map: O.S.Outdoor Leisure Sheet 14, Wye Valley & Forest of Dean

Start: The Dog and Muffler, Joyford. G.R. 578134

Access: Not the easiest pub in the world to find. From Coleford follow signs for Symonds Yat along the B4228. Having passed The Pike House pub (on your right at a crossroads) turn next right and stay with this road across several junctions (one marked by a closed pub). At the bottom of a short, steep hill turn right, the pub car park is half-left at the end of the short road.

From Ross-on-Wye take the Symond's Yat, Lydbrook and Coleford road (B4234) and stay with this through English Bicknor. Half a mile beyond the village the pub is signposted, left, at a grassy triangular junction beside Dryslade Farm.

Bus: Regular service 35 (not Sundays) to English Bicknor from Coleford and Ross-on-Wye

---

A couple of short, steep climbs, otherwise fairly easy going, visiting a hidden valley, an ancient church and one of the best areas for spotting deer.

The Dog and Muffler (0594 832444)

An idiosyncratic name, but one of long-standing and with no obvious explanation other than the painting on the weathered old pub sign. Recent work has seen the pub's capacity at least doubled, largely in the form of a conservatory-style dining area off the main bar and overlooking a beer garden.

The old core of the pub remains intact, however, a small outer room warmed by a roaring open fire giving access to the snug little bar area,

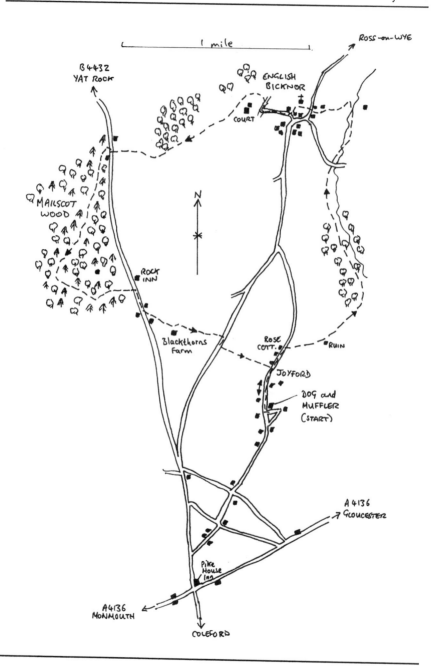

most of it reflected in the mirror which has formed the front of the bar itself for many a long year. Low beams, wall seats and a few small tables fill the space between bar and fireplace; sadly the old open fire succumbed during the renovations and new kitchen extension, a gas fire now filling the space.

You'll see several tiny bales of hay hanging from various beams throughout the pub, and in other pubs in this area. Two tales are given as reason for their presence, one that they dissipate tobacco smoke and act as a kind of air refreshener, the other that they are a good luck charm or omen, hung in the pub to ward off evil, witches and gipsy curses!

There's a separate games room and "public bar" formed out of an old barn and entered from the pub's back garden. This garden is dominated by an old cider mill, the type once powered by a donkey-in-harness, now filled with flowers rather than the seasonal apple crop. It's highly likely that this was once used in anger on the premises as old records show several cider makers active in the area, the old barn (now the public bar) being an ideal structure for use as the fermentation house. Plans are afoot to extend and improve this part of the pub, so by the time you read this the public bar may be considerably altered.

The excellent Sam Smiths Old Brewery Bitter has been on handpump here for at least twenty years, and I've never had a bad pint here during this lengthy stretch. More recently a second draught beer has been available, Ruddles County on my last visit. The food side of the business has also grown beyond recognition in the same timespan and the Dog now has an enviable reputation for the quality, range and size of its meals. Opening hours are 11 a.m. to 3 p.m. and 6 p.m. to 11 p.m., standard Sunday hours.

The Walk

Walk to the end of the pub's front garden (i.e. the beer garden beyond the new dining room) and turn right down the narrow road. Remain with this for a good half mile, gradually climbing up out of the shallow valley. The isolated white building down on your right was one of the local corn mills; long since disused as such, it's small millpond now dried up.

As the road bends slightly left just past Rose Cottage look on the right for the tall wooden-rail stile, beside a field gate and near a telegraph pole. Enter the field here and walk along the old trackway, passing by the old barn and gradually dropping down into a narrow, streamless valley.

To the left of one of the stiles you climb is a small shelter covering a winch and ladders leading down into the depths of a pothole. Presumably a local caving club accesses a series of caves and pots at this point. This is limestone country, where streams disappear underground for hundreds of yards (explaining the dry valley in which you are walking) only to re-emerge where a different rock type is encountered. Such streams contribute to dissolving away the limestone leaving the pots and caves far beneath the surface.

Remain with the path as it enters an area of very old woodland, the ancient oaks, hornbeam and lime bedecked with massive creepers and ivy. The obvious, rather muddy path meanders along the valley floor, at some point the stream re-emerges from a spring, coursing a lively way beneath matted layers of bramble and swathes of spring blooms. Follow this path alongside or above the stream to reach a narrow road and go straight over this, walking past old oaks and into the constricted valley. Aim for the tall scots pines and cross the stile, then the footbridge over the lively brook.

Follow the path beyond a stile, rising slightly above an area of tumbled masonry and hollows. This has recently been the site of an archaeological dig. What the subject matter is (was) is hard to discern. There are records of the sale of great quantities of cinders from English Bicknor several centuries ago, so this may possibly be the site of a medieval forge or furnace. Certainly an ancient routeway is shown on old maps as falling into the valley at this point.

At the far end of this area of ruins is an ages-old surfaced causeway leading to a crossing of the brook beneath a great lime tree. There are more old walls and dressed stones here, cross the fence beyond the stream via the upright slab, then look back-left up the very steep pasture to sight the tallest tree on the ridge top and walk up towards this. An old track gradually becomes discernible, leading up to the tree. Climb the stile beneath this and follow the walled track up into the small village of English Bicknor.

Walk through the churchyard, noting the substantial, rough old mound and hollows immediately south of the surrounding wall. These features are the remains of a large motte and bailey castle which once stood at this ridge end, commanding old routeways up the two adjoining valleys. St. Mary's Church itself has a long history, its foundation dating back to the same Norman baron who built the castle in about 1140 A.D. Inside are some fine effigy tombs including a splendid one of a priest.

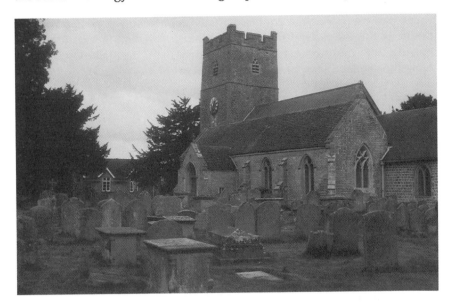

English Bicknor

Leave the churchyard via the gate beside the school and walk through the schoolyard to the right of the "Portacabin" classroom. Continue along the roadway beyond, then turn sharp right at the far end of the parking area and follow the lane gradually downhill away from the village.

At the junction turn right with the sign for Coldwell Walks then, within yards, bear left at the somewhat hidden footpath sign (attached to a telegraph pole) for "Coldwell Walk, footpath only." Work up this roughly stepped path through the edge of the woods, gnarled yew trees shading an undergrowth steeped with wildflowers, primroses, celandine, wild garlic and wood anemones thickly carpeting the thin soils of this limestone spur, Rosemary Topping.

At the far end of the woods walk through the horse pasture, part of the landholding of nearby Bicknor Court, the imposing village Manor House. A line of stiles leads through the long pastures above the top end of the woods, which here disguise the edge of the Wye Gorge, just a few yards into the trees. In a couple of spots there is sufficient gap through the trees to glimpse the famous viewpoint of Symonds Yat Rock, that buttress of limestone towering hundreds of feet above a great horseshoe-shaped loop of the Wye.

The pasture narrows to a track between the woods and a high hedge. Climb the stile beyond the ford and sweep right up into the open field beyond this neck of woodland. Keep with the line of the old tractor road up the field, the woods gradually falling away to the right as views open out across to Coppet Hill and across the Herefordshire plain. Shortly, join the line of a threadbare hedge/fence on your left and remain with this to the road. Turn right along this, then left in 30 yards or so. Don't go along the driveway towards the cottage named "Cervidae" but, rather, the forestry road beyond it, bearing left with the curve and entering the woods.

Remain with this roadway, going straight across at the crossing of tracks in the middle of a recently felled area. This activity has had the benefit of opening up views westwards across the hidden gorge of the Wye to Lord's Wood and Buckholt Wood across the nearby Welsh border. At the far side of this clearing, just past the stand of tall fir trees, the roadway splits at an enormous oak.

Bear right here, passing by a strangely isolated picnic table beside this forest track. The woods are close, on either side here, offering opportunity to find points where deer habitually cross the track; look for points opposite each other at the tracksides, marked by scuffed earth or muddy chutes and backed by narrow paths leading back into the woods. A closer look reveals hoofprints left in the banks as the timid creatures hurry from one thicket to the next. This area, Mailscot and Highmeadow Woods, is one of the most likely in which to see deer by chance rather than by design, so keep those eyes peeled!

In half a mile or so, as the roadway bends left, is a tall lone pine tree and a stand of oaks. At this point a wide grassy path diverges left from the forest road, a point marked by a red-waymarked post. This is the route to take, the woods on either side shading a panoply of bluebells and wild garlic in early spring. This quiet forest track is an excellent locale for birdwatchers. The thick fir woods to your left are home to crossbills and firecrest, Britain's smallest bird, whilst the older deciduous woods host all three species of woodpecker (Great Spotted, Lesser Spotted and Green), nuthatches, tree creepers, jays and nightjar.

The path eventually merges with another forestry road, simply bear left and walk gently uphill with it to the minor road. If all this birdwatching and deer spotting has worked up an irresistible thirst then, to the left here, The Rock Inn has a range of ales to put you to rights. If not, then bear right along the road, then angle left up the driveway before the telephone box, heading for Blackthorns Farm. Just before the farm go left into the camping field and turn right along the edge of the field. Pass through the gate at the far end and follow the line of hedge to your left.

Shortly after a stile the path passes by a small, grassed over old spoil tip, one of several in the area originating from the long-closed little Folly Colliery. A close look at the spoil reveals small sections of fossilised trees and stems.

The views from this modest little mound are spectacular. West (behind you) the distinctive shapes of the Skirrid and the Sugar Loaf, both near Abergavenny, pale beneath the heights of the Black Mountains; the highest point is the flat-topped knoll of Waun Fach at nearly 2700 feet. Further north the smudge on the horizon is Radnor Forest in mid-Wales whilst virtually due north is the sharp peak and sudden edge of the Clee Hills in Shropshire. Completing this distant sweep, before the Forest makes the near horizon, are the rounded humps of the Malvern Hills, amongst the oldest hills in Britain.

Walk beyond this spoil tip to the road and turn right. In about thirty yards go left at the footpath sign and walk along the edge of two fields to the minor road beside the white cottage. Turn right along the road to return to Joyford and the weathered old sign for the Dog and Muffler.

17. Newland

Route: Redbrook – Whitecliff – Newland

Distance: 8 miles

Map: O.S. Outdoor Leisure Sheet 14, Wye Valley and Forest of Dean.

Start: The Bush Inn, Redbrook. G.R. SO 535102

Access: Redbrook is in the Wye Valley, about 3 miles south of Monmouth on the A466. The Bush is beside this road at the north of the village. There's a small car park (up the road to Clearwell), and roadside parking opposite.

Bus: Regular daily (except Sundays) service 69, approx. every two hours from Monmouth and Chepstow; there's a stop outside the pub.

A walk with several moderate/easy climbs, passing by many relics of bygone industrial times and visiting probably Dean's most spectacular church and oldest pub.

The Bush Inn (0600 713237)

A wide selection of old railway photographs and prints recall the days when The Bush was virtually an abutment of a bridge carrying the old Wye Valley Railway from Redbrook to Monmouth; the line closed in early 1964 but the bridge remained for many years.

The pub has changed little since those days, only fairly recently were the two main public rooms combined into the comfortable establishment to be found today, the beams and forest stone walls now freed from the all-covering plaster of years past. One framed document on the wall records the pub up for sale in 1899.

The Bush strives successfully to be both a local's den and walker's watering hole (Offa's Dyke Path and the Wye Valley Way both run past its door), all-day opening (standard hours on Sundays) ensuring a good turnover of beers and very well kept Marston's Pedigree, Brain's Bitter and Hook Norton Bitter. Sadly Redbrook Ales, brewed in the old brewery virtually opposite the pub, are now but a wistful memory. Bar food and basket meals are available all day, the huge choice includes venison pie.

The Walk

Redbrook is nowadays no more than a strand of houses and cottages along the east bank of the River Wye and two tributary streams. Hard to imagine that this was one of the world's leading tinplate centres a century ago; only a few scant remains now stand in Lower Redbrook, the works finally succumbing in 1961. These tinplate works developed from copperworks for which the village was equally renowned in the early 1700s.

The village's two deep, winding valleys also housed many corn mills, flour mills, iron foundries and two iron furnaces, one of which was a very early convert to coke-smelting (in 1716, the process only having been developed by Abraham Darby in Coalbrookdale, Shropshire, in 1709).

Turn left up the pub-side road towards Newland and Clearwell, shortly passing beneath a steeply inclined bridge. This is the route of the Monmouth tramroad which once connected Forest quarries, iron ore and coal pits with the Wye navigation in the early 1800s (opened in 1813); its arms and branches snaked between Coleford, Redbrook and Monmouth. Its real claim to fame, though, and almost totally unsung, is that it was the first railed-way in the world specifically to make provision (in taking its Parliamentary powers) to carry, and to charge a fare to, passengers. Supporters of the Oystermouth Railway (near Swansea) and the Liverpool and Manchester Railway both energetically claim this land-mark as their own, but it was this short-lived backwater of a line which first took that significant step. The incline here at Redbrook transferred wagons from the main level, high above the Bush Inn, down to riverside wharves and to the tinplate works.

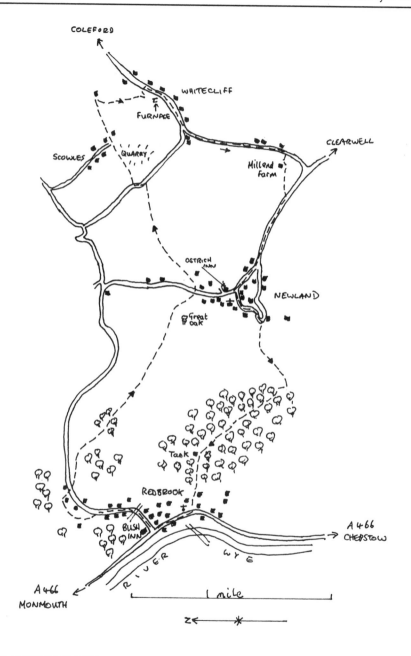

On your right is a substantial old wheel pit next to Mill Cottage, another reminder of the extensive industries that once filled these Forest-edge valleys. By their names various nearby cottages recall the existence of one of Redbrook's breweries in this narrow valley.

Continue up the minor road and remain with it for about 400 yards to the footpath on the left, signposted for Monmouth and marked with an acorn, the logo of the Offa's Dyke Path of which the next few hundred yards is a part. The track quickly gains height affording views down over old millponds and converted cottages and behind over the Wye Valley to Tintern Forest. For a short distance here you're in Wales (Gwent), the Red Brook is, for nearly a mile, the Wales/England border.

Pass by the drive to Cobbs Tump and follow the track round past the green painted cottage on your right. Shortly after this a concrete pipe is partially buried in the track – it acts as a kind of sleeping policeman. Here turn sharp right and plunge down the sunken track beneath the bower of trees, passing behind the green cottage to reach a minor road at the bottom. Virtually opposite you here is a footpath sign pointing the way down to a slat-bridge over the stream, once across which climb steeply to the stile at the top, then follow the direction of the waymark arrow half left up across the valleyside pasture.

Go over the stile in the top left corner and follow the path through the scrubby woodland. From the next stile walk slightly left across the field aiming for the ivy-covered trees. Look out on your left for a metal field gate just up from the edge of the wood (and below the ivy-clad trees) beside which is a stile to cross. Stick to the fence on your right, cross the stile in this fence and turn left, keeping the trees on your left.

Continue along the line of waymarkers, crossing stiles as necessary. About 30 yards beyond the stile next to the old tree stump cross the stile on the left and turn right, then follow the line of hedge. In the field on the right is the ancient Newland Oak (q.v.). Newland itself is now visible in the distance, with a welcome awaiting at the sign of The Ostrich if you've already worked up a thirst!

To reach the village climb the gate at the bottom, pass by the water trough on your right and leave the hedgerow at the corner, following the obvious track across the pasture towards the white cottage at the far side. If you want to visit the Ostrich now, turn right along the road. If not, cross the road here and walk up through the parking area to the left of this, Newland Cottage. Go through the small gate at the back and then over the stile which is almost immediately on your left. Head diagonally across this small paddock to the kissing gate on the far side and then go straight across the track and climb the stile beyond.

This track was the course of the old Great Western Railway between Monmouth and Coleford, lifted as long ago as 1915 to allow use of the rails on the ephemeral railways of the Western Front. In many places this G.W.R. branch had been laid on the route of the original old tramroad.

Cross the pasture to the stile in the hedge, climb this and then look to the right hand edge of the field and aim just to the left of the tall oak tree at the end of a line of trees in the hedge. Cross the stile here and turn three-quarters left to find a stile about 20 yards up the left hand side of this field. Once over this head three-quarters right up the field, crest the brow and walk to the stile at the right hand end of the tall thorn hedge. Go straight across the old lane here and down along the track directly opposite, shortly reaching a minor road.

Turn left up the road to reach the public footpath sign on the right about 30 yards uphill, climbing up to and over the stile here and then following the line of the tall hedge on your right. Climb the stile at the top and walk along the narrow path, the wire fence on the right marking the edge of a vast old sandstone/limestone quarry. At the end of the path join the surfaced road and walk ahead-right along to the cottages. Follow the tarred footpath between the cottage gardens, pass through the substantial green metal gate and walk along the tarred path beyond, marking the very edge of Coleford's Recreation Grounds.

Take the footpath signposted off to the right just before the small works, climb the stile at the end and walk across the field to a further stile beside the wooden electricity pole. Go over this, walk ahead for a few yards and then walk off at a tangent to the left, walking down the steep pasture to the far left hand corner where a waymarker directs you to the old railway track. Cross straight over this to the wooden fencing, enter the small pasture here and turn sharp left, following the path downhill.

Look down to the right to the white-painted Whitecliff Cottage and aim to join the minor road at this point. Turn right and walk downhill. On your right is the substantial Whitecliff Furnace, a Scheduled Monument undergoing sporadic repair and preservation as a leading example of an early coke-fired iron furnace.

Remain with this road for nearly a mile, following it left around the sharp bend where the narrower High Meadow Lane branches to the right. One of the cottages here was the holiday home of James Keir Hardie, the first leader of the Parliamentary Labour Party (1906).

Continue down the main road, look on the right for, and go down, the drive towards Millend Farm. Bear left before you reach the cultivated garden, walk across the rough pasture and climb the stile which is a few yards to the left of the house. Head half right to the small mound, capped by trees, half way up the far side of the field, climb the stile here and head half left across the subsequent field to the rough wooden stile in the hedge. Climb this and turn right along the road to the tiny village of Newland.

The village is dominated by All Saints Church, a massive medieval structure known as the Cathedral of the Forest which houses several good relief-tombs and the tiny Miner's Brass (the brass, not the miner...), said to be the only medieval brass dedicated to a commoner.

Restorations undertaken about 130 years ago left the building refreshingly unaltered, virtually unheard of during Victorian times. The huge churchyard is bordered by old almshouses, established by one William Jones, a local son made good in the London haberdashery trade in the early 1600s, and substantial gentleman's residences.

It contains some very old and unusual gravestones; one, to Jenkin Wyrall, a fifteenth century forester whose panelled tomb depicts him dressed in his garb of Lincoln Green, as it were, has been moved inside to retard the effects of weathering. Virtually next door is the old church farm with its ancient barn, a sprinkling of late-medieval and Georgian houses and mansions all but complete the stock of this glorious, unsung little settlement.

One village resident, almost as old as the Church, retains but a vestige of life. This is the Great Oak of Newland, once one of England's premier oaks. Standing in a field to the north of the village, the hollow, gnarled remains can be seen from the walk, still managing to produce a few shoots and twigs each spring despite having been all-but destroyed by a freak gale and snowstorm in the summer of 1955. Its age has been estimated at nearly 700 years, at one time its girth of over forty-six feet was claimed as the greatest in all England. A sapling raised from one of its acorns was planted nearby in the 1970s to continue its proud lineage.

The village Inn, The Ostrich, is as unchanging a pub as you'll find anywhere. Parts of it date back to the Thirteenth Century, even the new bits are 350 years old. From the cosy little bar may be purchased an ever changing selection of real ales. This is a delightful little pub to savour, if you hit Newland during licensing hours miss it at your peril.

The Ostrich, Newland

Leave the churchyard at the southwest corner (the opposite corner to that near The Ostrich) and walk down the steep, narrow road. Turn right at the bottom and walk along to the end, ignoring the left hand fork.

Walk as far as you can go, past the yard to your left, and go up the narrow, sunken track which is well hidden in the trees ahead – there may be a brook flowing down it. Walk up this to its end. Off to the left the broad, steep-sided valley marks the former course of the River Wye, over 200 feet above the present river, perhaps the most impressive of the abandoned meanders of this ancient river, its course now mimicked by the tiny Valley Brook which flows down to Redbrook, once being utilised to power waterwheels and turbines for the industries there.

From the clearing at the end of the sunken track take the second exit on the right, a forestry road that descends slowly down through the trees. Remain with this for about half a mile until you reach a large water tank at a split in the track.

Bear left at this fork and follow this track, favouring the steepest option at subsequent junctions and picking up the tarmaced roadway which soon brings you back to Redbrook village. Turn right along the main road to return to The Bush Inn.

18. The Heart of the Forest

Route: Moseley Green – New Fancy – Staple Edge – Danby Lodge

Distance: 7 miles

Map: O.S. Outdoor Leisure Sheet 14, Wye Valley & Forest of Dean

Start: The Rising Sun, Moseley Green. G.R. SO 632086

Access: Take the Blakeney road from Parkend and follow it for about two miles, passing by (left) the turn to Speech House. Soon after this turn right by the old, renovated chapel, the pub is a further half mile along this road, off to the right – look for the home-made signboard.

A pleasant walk almost entirely along forestry roads and woodland paths. Several short, very steep climbs.

The Rising Sun (0594 562008)

A basic but welcoming pub, hugely popular with forest recreationalists, it can have changed little since the days when half a dozen or so major coalmines and quarries were working no more than a stones throw from the front door.

Perhaps the main difference is that coal dust on the linoleum floors has given way to mud. The old industrial days are recalled by a collection of old notices and advertisements concerning sales of mines, coal, stone, etc. dotted around the walls of the pub's considerable interior. Still on an industrial theme, the pub's only signs of kitsch are the reproduction miner's Davy Lamps which act as lighting for much of the interior.

It makes the most of its woodland situation, with massive beer gardens to two sides, one dedicated more-or-less to children (with swings, etc.), the other beside a huge goldfish pond, more of a small lake really, at the edge of the encroaching forest. Weekends, high days and holidays see the place heaving with groups of walkers and umpteen mountain bikers (I'm not aware of the correct collective noun for mountain bikers, maybe an erosion of mountain bikers may be appropriate?). All make the most of the range of bar meals, the Flowers Original Bitter and the gravity-drawn cider available at the bar.

The Walk

Turn right from the pub's back door (i.e. the main entrance, opposite the fishpond) and walk away from the building in line with this back wall. Continue straight across the top of the drive and along the green path (virtually opposite the cellar entrance) into the woods. At the crossing of paths, about 200 yards along, turn left along the wider track and walk gradually uphill.

Go straight over the next crossing of paths, at which place the fir trees give way to deciduous woodland, and continue to the small car park at the end. Walk to the road here and go along the road opposite, signposted for Speech House and Cinderford.

Opposite the bus shelter bear right along the forestry road, in a few yards climb the stile beside the gateway (rather than continuing to the houses visible in the middle distance) and follow this well used roadway through the forest.

When you reach, on your left, the waymark post with a red "1" on it, take a few minutes to go along this path to the viewpoint and picnic site at New Fancy. This has been created from the old New Fancy Colliery, one of the largest in Dean's coalfield; at its height it employed well over 700 people, it closed in 1944. Thirty and more years later the Forestry Commission landscaped the old spoil tip and laid out the viewing area at the top, about 600 feet above sea level. Views can be considerable, across great tracts of, largely, conifers to the edges of the plateau; the view SW is best, across Bream to St. Briavels and, beyond this, the heights of Trellech Beacon, that great wooded tump on the far side of the hidden Wye gorge.

Return to the forestry road and continue northeast. At the junction by the large lime tree take the right hand fork and stay with this wider roadway to reach a crossroads marked by a stand of Scots pines and a

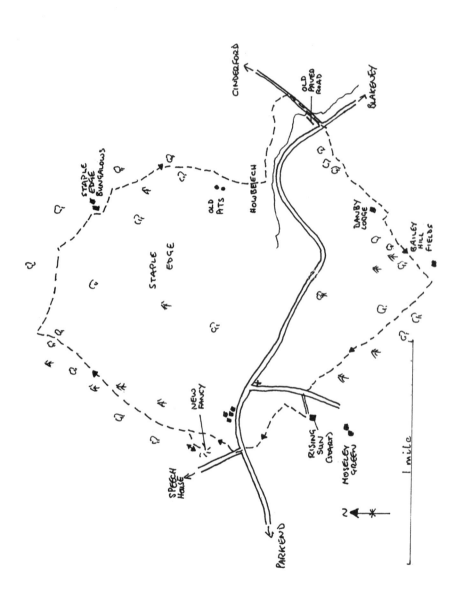

"3" waymark post. Here go straight ahead and up along the narrower, very muddy path which almost immediately steepens, uphill. To your right beside this very cloyey-underfoot path is a supreme example of the dark, lifeless atmosphere created beneath the thick plantations of Sitka spruce, Norway spruce and the other fast-growing species which make up the majority of the plantations hereabouts.

The path narrows and bends slightly left through a grove of beech and oak trees. Ignore the waymark to the left here, instead continuing to the crossing of paths a short distance further on. Turn right here and slide down the treacherously muddy path to the forestry road at the bottom. Go virtually straight across this and along the path indicated by a yellow arrow painted on an old wooden post.

Cross the brook and commence the long, steady haul up Staple Edge, shortly passing beneath a line of electricity cables. On your right in the mixed, mature woods you may see several tall pines lying on their sides having been felled by high winds. Their wide but shallow root systems thus exposed show why they are a favourite species for planting on poor soils, or on reclamation sites such as old colliery tips.

Beyond the great, felled and cleared area on your left an undulating range of hilltops penetrate the horizon above the treetops in the distance. These are the grassed-over "coal alps" of the old Lightmoor Colliery near Cinderford, amongst the last remaining in Dean which haven't been either removed or afforested. The path becomes enclosed by trees again, go over the offset stile onto the forestry road at the top and then up the dark path into the thicker woodland opposite, indicated by another painted yellow arrow, this one on a flash cut into a tree.

The path steepens before reaching the ridge of Staple Hill near an isolated pair of bungalows. Bear right along the outside of the hedge, then go left as this meets the forestry road and walk down this. Ahead, the nick in the trees allows distant views to the line of the Cotswolds. In about 150 yards go right, along the grassy path marked by a yellow arrow painted on a small beech tree. Stay with this fairly obvious path to reach a crossing of paths and a forestry road.

Here bear slightly left to follow the narrow, bracken-lined path alongside young oaks and more mature beeches on your left. In a while the path steepens and falls through an area shorn of all trees except tall, willowy Spanish Chestnuts, creating a great semi-clearing in the forest.

The path ends by joining a wide forestry road at an acute angle. The route to take now is along the green track which leaves the roadway at a similarly shallow angle opposite, in fifty yards or so plunging out of the clearing and into thicker woodland.

Spare a moment, though, to follow the forestry road downhill for a few yards where, off to the right, you'll find several old freemines, the waste tips somewhat overgrown and the entrances to the adits boarded up and infilled. This is written in mid-1992, such is the nature of these mines that by the time you do this walk these small mines may once again be in operation.

Continuing down the green track, fir woods once again appear to your left whilst on your right is a splendid example of coppiced woodland, the boles of the chestnut trees sprouting off many thinner branches and shoots from their trunks. This deepening valley is Howbeech Slade, a tramroad once ran along this, linking workings in the area with the G.W.R. branch which followed the main valley a little to the south.

Bear left with the greatly widening, muddy path to reach a further forestry road. At this point turn sharp left and pick up this well surfaced road, a welcome relief from the muddy section just completed. This is a very pleasant stretch of the walk, great banks of deciduous woods rolling away ahead as you gradually fall down into the valley of the Blackpool Brook, the road bordered with swathes of colourful gorse and broom and the hillside to your left dotted with fallen boulders beneath majestic oaks, beeches, hornbeams and chestnuts.

On reaching the minor road turn right and follow it over the stream at Wenchford. Here you'll find a stretch of what has long been described as Roman Road exposed to the elements, a length of roughly cobbled carriageway bounded by kerbing and ditches.

Recent work has proved that the road, as visible, is only about 300 years old, but it undoubtedly follows much the same line as the supposed Roman Road between Ariconium (near Ross-on-Wye) and the Severn near Lydney, "The Dean Road." Just before the main road, the bridge under which you pass once carried the short-lived Forest of Dean Central Railway, linking New Fancy Colliery with the main line at Awre Junction.

Abandoned Freemine, Howbeech Slade

"Roman" road at Blackpool Bridge

Go straight across the main road and to the barrier across the forestry road opposite. Immediately past this go up the path to the right, winding up this steep main path to a wider track some way uphill, here bearing right with the red waymarker. Continue along this track to the forestry road and go virtually straight across this, up the very steep path indicated by the red waymark post. This levels out as it joins a wider path virtually along the ridgetop of Bailey Hill, a junction marked by an enormous beech tree sporting, in autumn, large growths of bracket and other fungi.

Walk along this wider path, the wall to your right surrounding the isolated house, Danby Lodge. Very shortly this path emerges at a complicated junction of roads and paths near the end of the drive to Danby Lodge. Cross the main forestry road and head a fraction right, aiming for this end of the line of tall cupressor trees and, nearby, telegraph pole 51. Follow the grassy path alongside the woods and with the open pastures on your left, about a quarter of a mile's walk brings you to a forestry road, a few yards past the point where the fence curved left towards another isolated cottage. At the far side of the road a wire fence blocks further progress (notwithstanding the stile further to your left).

Turn right here and walk downhill with this roadway, following the line of wooden pylons. Simply go straight across any crossroads, staying with these pylons to the point where they bend right, off the main roadway and into the trees. Here, continue straight ahead up the increasingly muddy track, eventually emerging on the minor road at Moseley Green virtually opposite the roadway leading to The Rising Sun.

19. Oakwood

Route: Sling – Clearwell – Stowe Green – Bearse – Oakwood

Distance: 6 miles

Map: O.S. Outdoor Leisure Sheet 14, Wye Valley & Forest of Dean

Start: The Orepool Inn, Sling. G.R. SO 579076

Access: Sling is about three miles south of Coleford on the B4228 road to St. Briavels and Lydney. The pub is beside this road, immediately south of the hamlet.

Bus: Infrequent Monday to Friday service N3 runs from Coleford Square and Lydney Bus Station to Sling village, about a quarter mile from the Orepool.

A gentle walk largely through the pastureland of the high Forest, culminating in a fine wooded stretch hiding industrial remains dating back two millenia.

The Orepool (0594 833277)

Over the past decade or so this pub has mutated from a small old roadside alehouse to a considerable motel complex with all its attendant facilities. Nonetheless, the old pub remains intact at the heart of the development, the several small rooms as you enter the building retaining the old beams, fireplaces, nooks, crannies and panelling of years gone by; if you use the small side bar you can all-but ignore the huge extensions tacked onto the back and the rather brash font-taps which dispense numerous lagers.

Thankfully several handpumps remain, dispensing Theakstons, Bass and a number of draught ciders to thirsting ramblers, all day (11 a.m. – 11 p.m.) every day (Sundays 12 – 2.30 p.m., 7 – 10.30 p.m.); bar meals are available throughout. There's a huge beer garden behind the pub.

The original pub is about 350 years old, built beside an ancient trade route (in all probability a Roman one), The Oreway, developed to ease transport of iron ore from the numerous workings which existed until earlier this century. Old Sling mine was only yards away from the Inn, the nearest railway line just a few hundred yards to the north at Clearwell Meend, near the Miners Arms (also open all day, selling "Miners Bitter"). The name "Orepool" is held to derive from the practice of medieval (or earlier) miners "pooling" their ore for sale in bulk to dealers and traders who would meet at or near the site.

The Walk

An old barn stands virtually opposite the pub; take the footpath signposted along the side of this and drop gently into the narrow dry valley, a sure sign that this is limestone country. At the bottom end of the second field, as this valley deepens, is a choice of stiles. Go for the one on the right, climbing the stile to the right of the metal field gate and follow the path along the edge of the spinney and gradually down the valley. Continue beyond the woods and walk along the rough pasture, skirting the right of the graveyard wall to reach a minor road at the edge of the village of Clearwell.

A short detour up the road to the right here brings you to "Clearwell Caves," the former Old Ham Iron Mine now seeing a new lease of life as a leading industrial museum, the old caves and mined chambers utilised to explain the story of Dean's ore/ochre mining industry. Eight underground chambers are open to visitors in this fascinating museum, open daily from March to October (inclusive).

Otherwise, turn left and wind down into Clearwell, a small village of ancient cottages hugging lanes which dive down from the plateau following the twisting valleys cut by streams in ages past. The clear well of its name issues behind the Wyndham Arms, at the village centre near the medieval cross.

The settlement has a proud industrial history, hosting nail-makers, a tannery, ore and ochre mines, all now long gone although the rusting skeletons of old quarry buildings still stand in woodland northeast of the village.

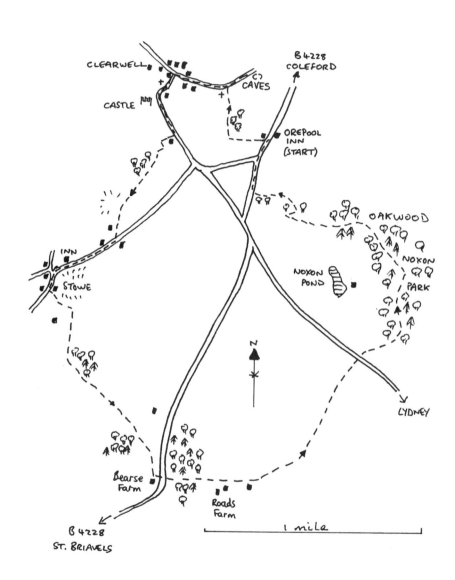

The village's largest building, Clearwell Castle, is a gothic-style extravaganza built in 1727 for the Wyndham family on the site of the medieval manor house. It was severely damaged by fire early this century, but has risen phoenix-like to become a smart hotel, you get but glimpses of it hidden behind the high estate walls. The nearby Victorian church, St. Peters, is worth visiting to experience the great array of sandstones, limestones, marbles and serpentine used in its interior decoration.

From the cross take the road towards Lydney, walking uphill alongside a stretch of the castle walls for a short distance. About ten yards before the speed de-restriction sign go right along the signposted footpath and follow the walled pathway around this pasture and the back of Platwell House Farm.

The finger of woodland to your right all but hides Clearwell Castle, nestling in its tiny valley amidst a small area of parkland. Continue beyond the end of the woods, gradually gaining height alongside the wall. This increasing altitude opens out views to the left (east) to the Cotswold Hills and west to the line of the Black Mountains, the eastern edge of the Brecon Beacons National Park.

The ever-expanding Clearwell Quarry now appears on your right. The developers, Tilcon, have planted a veritable forest of young trees which in time will help disguise the workings. The effect of the quarry spreads even beyond the boundary fence, most of the angular pieces of rock which pepper the fields through which you are walking have almost certainly been thrown out during blasting operations in years past. Many have been split open revealing a rich variety of fossil shells. The last field you enter has a ruined barn in one corner, bear half-left across this field and follow the line of electricity cables to gain a minor road, turning right along this.

Walk past the Traveller's Rest (or not as the fancy takes you...) here in Stowe hamlet and follow the main road around the corner. Within yards, pass by on your left the entrance to the quarry. Immediately beyond this go left over the cattle-grid and up the roadway for a few yards, then go ahead up the pasture, fence and quarry on your left. On reaching the fence climb the waymarked stile on the right and walk along the edge of the field to the wedge of woodland ahead.

At the far side of the trees, climb the stile on the left and walk along the woodland edge. The village on the hilltop off to your right is St. Briavels, its medieval castle hidden behind the trees above which pokes the tower of the church. Climb the stile at the corner and bear half-right across the subsequent field, heading for the near end of the funnel of trees which mark the steep valley of the infant Slade Brook.

At the head of this defile is a small old quarry, little more than a pit from which, no doubt, the stone to build the nearby old barn and farm was dug. The very friable rocks here are, again, full of bivalve fossils whilst the small, round fossils are sections of the stems of crinoids, a kind of sea lily.

Climb the stile between these diggings and the woods and head in the direction indicated by the arrow across a line of stiles towards the corrugated iron barn in the distance. In the near corner of the farmyard look carefully on your left for the waymarked stiles and scramble up to the road, crossing straight over this and following the drive along to Roads Farm. The woodland edges here are incredibly rich with wildflowers, particularly great clumps of primroses in spring and mayflowers in April and May.

Continue on past the farm and stick with the road as it becomes a rough lane. About 100 yards past the stone-built Roads House (on your right) go through the wide, turquoise field gate on your left and follow the direction indicated by the waymark arrow, heading directly towards the transmitter on the distant hilltop.

At the far corner of the field climb the succession of stiles through the rough hollow (marked on old maps as Broadfield Pond, so in the wettest of weathers it may be marshy) and on reaching the open field beyond head diagonally across it to reach a stile and, beyond this, the main Lydney road. Go straight across this, through the gate opposite and walk along the line of the hedge on your right.

Off to the left is Noxon Farm and, beyond this, the sheet of water is Noxon Pond. This is partially an area of flooded old scowles, ancient opencast pits dug in medieval times by miners following lodes of iron ore. Similar remains can be found in the woods the walk now enters.

Climb the stile and follow the wide track through the mixed fir and broadleaf woods, a thick growth of ramsons adding their pungent smell as well as carpet of white flowers throughout the spring months. Almost immediately, areas of shallow diggings are evident just yards away from this track. At the crossing of tracks turn left, following this northwards through a great area of scowles, now comprehensively overgrown with creepers and mature trees, many of them hazels showing signs of coppicing in years gone by.

The track winds down a shallow side-valley to emerge in a large clearing, the bottom of the valley of Oakwood Brook. Bear left here and walk up this long clearing, a line of tall firs off to your right. The valley is peaceful now but in mid-Victorian times it supported a thriving industrial community.

Here were the important China Engine, Oakwood Mill and Princess Louise iron mines, a foundry and furnace; a little further down stood a cornmill, a wood-distillation works and a pub, the Oakwood Inn, all served by a tramroad. Scant remains exist of any of these, the forest having largely reclaimed its own. Hard to credit that this sylvan landscape saw nearly half-a-million tons of iron ore extracted from beneath its roots during Victoria's reign.

Leave the clearing via the stile/gate near the large beech trees at the north-west corner and follow the obvious grassy track up the wide valley, soon passing by a deep, narrow old quarry on your left and ignoring the waymarks pointing right through the larches. At one point an ancient beech has fallen in a gale, many new shoots and branches climbing from this fallen host towards the sky producing a most unusually shaped tree. To your left the narrow mill leat, or goit, is the sole reminder of the industries of yesteryear.

Climb the stile out of the woods and head for the far right-hand corner of the field, where a waymark directs you right, up through a wedge of rather tattered woodland. In about 50 yards, and before you reach the field gate, look up to the left to find a stile out of the woods, once over which climb the further stile immediately on the left and aim to walk well to the left of the electricity pylon which pokes its top over the near horizon. Cross the hump of the hill and head for the line of old, ivy-covered ash trees, following this line to the road. Turn right along this and walk the last quarter of a mile back to the Orepool.

20. St. Briavels Common

Route: Brockweir – Coed Ithel – Hudnalls – St. Briavels Common

Distance: 6 miles

Map: O.S. Outdoor Leisure Sheet 14, Wye Valley & Forest of Dean

Start: Brockweir.

Access: Brockweir is in the Wye Valley between Monmouth and Chepstow, rather closer to the latter. Parking in the hamlet is difficult, far better to park in the large lay-by beside the A466 just north of the bridge and walk back to Brockweir across this bridge.

Bus: Service 69 runs approx. every two hours, Monday to Saturday, between Monmouth and Chepstow, passing by the end of Brockweir Bridge.

A long, continual climb through oakwoods from the Wye to the heights of Dean, rewarded by superb views over the Severn and Wye. Includes a section of Offa's Dyke Path and an old shipbuilding centre.

The Brockweir Country Inn (0291 689548)

A truly splendid little old pub which once marketed its own bitter (brewed by Whitbread), its fare is nowadays a continually changing array of delights (Arkells, Tim Taylors, Smiles, Bass, etc., etc.) with regular doses of Wye Valley Bitter (brewed in Hereford) and Hook Norton Bitter. Of the two small bars the lounge to the right is the most convivial (the other is largely given over to pool and pub games), wall seats tucked into inglenooks and odd corners increasing the available space between the bar and the great stone fireplace.

Some of the beams were rescued from an old trow built at the river port in the 1800s, otherwise there are surprisingly few reminders of the hamlet's maritime history on display, instead old shotguns and a display of cartridge cases stand out from the more usual brasses and prints.

There are in evidence, however, reminders of the natural resources of the Wye, including a salmon putch reclining in one corner and an eel trap suspended from a beam. Brockweir was always one of the favourite spots at which to catch elvers (baby eels), although the apparently prohibitive cost of a permit seems to have decimated this practice.

There's a small beer garden behind the pub, hanging above the Mork Brook and a stones throw from the picturesque village chapel. The Inn has an excellent reputation for its food. It's open from 11.30 a.m. – 3 p.m. and 7 p.m. – 11 p.m.

Brockweir

Spend a few minutes savouring the atmosphere of this peaceful little hamlet before setting out along the riverbank. It seems as unlikely a place as you could find to have hosted what was once a locally important shipbuilding centre providing work for hundreds and hosting two dozen and more drinking establishments. Vessels of up to 300 tons were built here, from where they set sail all over the world, many were recorded on voyages to the West Indies, China and Australia.

The last ships were built in the 1840s, thereafter ship repairing remained a major employer for several decades. Today the only tangible remains are a small old quay and a propeller decorating the garden of an old riverside house. A chance discovery in 1967 recalled former days of glory. The remains of a small steamboat, "La Belle Marie," were exposed in the silt by the Quay during restoration work. This 31 ton vessel was built in Gloucester in 1866 and spent many years on cross-Bristol Channel ferry services between Somerset and Glamorgan before being retired to pleasure cruises on the Wye.

Long before the shipbuilding boom, the hamlet was a vital transhipment point for Forest iron ore, carried to the riverside by pack mule or wagon and transferred to ships for carriage to, amongst other places, Ireland. Traffic to the hamlet included wines and spices destined for the Constable of the Forest at St. Briavels Castle. One of his duties was to prevent the poaching of the King's Venison, a job at which he and his staff were less than successful, in the Middle Ages Brockweir apparently had a reputation amongst the merchants of Bristol as an easy place to obtain ready supplies of poached venison. Another recorded import was

The Brockweir Country Inn

kelp (seaweed) which was a favoured fertilizer in centuries past. Just behind the Inn a winding streamside path leads to the solid Moravian Church, a whitewashed building built in 1833.

The latticed cast-iron bridge was erected in 1906. Before that date a number of ferrymen (including, no doubt, the owner of La Belle Marie) made a good living in the village, enhanced in 1874 when a station was opened on the new railway line on the opposite bank of the Wye to the village. The cross-river fare was one (old) penny.

The Walk

Return to the riverbank by the bridge and walk along The Quay, the Wye on your left. The name hints at the former function of this area and here are the only vestiges of the old port. Continue along the concreted pathway, here the lower route of Offa's Dyke Path, constricted here and there by growths of the voracious Japanese Knotweed. The concrete soon peters out to leave a pleasant riverside stroll through riverside meadows guarded, initially, by a line of great copper beech trees.

Remain with the river for about a mile and a half. The large house on the Welsh side (the Wye here acts as the England/Wales border) is Catchmays Court. There's been a house on the site since at least the early 1600s when a local ironmaster, Sir Richard Cachemay, was resident, cutting timber for charcoaling from the English side of the Wye and using it in his furnace at Coed Ithel on the Welsh side. Some remains of this furnace still stand in the woods beyond the nearby, higher house.

Eventually you'll reach a point where the woods come down to the river, a point marked by a fence and stile. Don't climb this, instead walk up to the right to the point where the woodside barbed wire fence is tempered by a wrapping of old fertiliser bag. This marks the start of a path up through the forest so clamber over and walk up through the tall undergrowth. This soon peters out, bear slightly left to find a waymark arrow pointing through a gap in the old fence and up an initially ill-defined path through the trees.

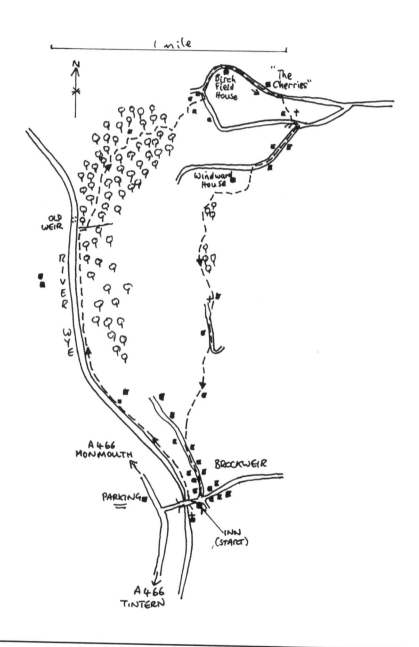

This becomes increasingly more obvious the higher you climb, in places bordered by sections of fallen wall. This marks it out as a long-established routeway from the heights above to the Wye, no doubt used in the past by employees of the shipbuilders at Brockweir. The path joined the riverbank at a point just below the long-gone Coed Ithel Weir; perhaps, too, Wye trows dropped some of their cargo here before proceeding upstream through the flash-lock which bypassed each weir (and there were many) on the river.

At the first fork, take the right-hand, upper path and continue up through the sun-dappled woodland, crossing several small brooks on rough stepping stones and increasingly bordered by fallen walls. The path emerges at the edge of an overgrown garden beside an isolated cottage. Don't walk out onto the garden, instead turn sharply-right back on yourself and walk for a few paces, then take the steep but obvious path on your left.

Cross the rough driveway and continue up the woodland path beyond, leaving the cottage down to your left. The woodlands hereabouts were renowned for their production of staves and of hoops, the latter used for barrel making, many cargoes of such were recorded from Brockweir to Chepstow, Bristol and other local towns.

Continue the climb, a wall now continuously on your left. Ignore any gaps in this and walk up to a major junction of paths. Keep left here and follow the wide, well worn track which winds through old walled areas of rough pasture and woodland, eventually joining the driveway to a cottage off to your right. Keep left, left again at the junction to pass a cottage on your left and remain with the drive to the end, whereupon turn left along the minor road.

At the junction bear right and follow this upper route of Offa's Dyke Path, soon leaving this to fall through fields whilst you continue past the imposing Birch Field House. To the left are extensive views up the Wye Valley over Bigsweir Bridge and up towards Monmouth.

This back lane climbs quite steeply up through the pastures at the edge of St. Briavels Common. About 75 yards past the house called "The Cherries" on your left bear right along the grassy walled track, cutting through to a small chapel. It's now a church for followers of the Gideon

Brockweir

persuasion, purveyors of bibles to the world's hotel industry, but originated as a school in 1852. Continue along the surfaced back road and turn second right, just beyond the bus shelter and signposted for Brockweir.

Wind round with this for about a quarter of a mile, looking on the left for the driveway to "Windward House." Turn along this rough lane and walk around the crest of the hill, obviously ignoring the subsequent drive to the house itself. As you pass round this southern aspect of Hudnalls Hill (at about 840 feet one of the highest points in Dean) great views are revealed over the lower Wye Valley and across the Severn Estuary to the rippled hills of the Cotswolds.

When you reach the County Council signpost turn left off this lane and join the narrow walled path (don't make the mistake of following the arrow straight ahead, this guides walkers coming up Offa's Dyke). In a hundred yards or so, bear right with the Offa's Dyke Path waymarker and follow this partially wooded path gradually downhill. Along this section, the actual line of Offa's Dyke is being followed, although it's all but impossible to discern any structure in the trees or undergrowth.

The path emerges onto tarmac near an old chapel, long converted into a private cottage, a few yards beyond which bear left at the junction and continue downhill.

At the sharp left hand bend go ahead down the "No through road" and as this horseshoes right go left along the path which leaves the head of this horseshoe. Immediately before you reach the modern white-painted house on the right turn right along the short, rather overgrown path outside the garden, then go virtually straight across the lane at the end, your route marked by an orange waymark arrow. This winds down through woodland to join another surfaced lane, turning left along which has you back at The Brockweir Inn in a quarter of a mile.

21. Old Bargains Wood

Route: Bream – Broom Hill – Old Bargains Wood – Scowles

Distance: 5 miles

Map: O.S. Outdoor Leisure Sheet 14, Wye Valley & Forest of Dean

Start: The Village Inn, Bream. G.R. SO 603058

Access: Bream lies off the Coleford to Lydney road about four miles NW of Lydney. It is well signposted from many parts of the central Forest area. The Village Inn is on High Street, opposite the War Memorial.

Bus: Infrequent N3 service runs Monday to Friday from Coleford and Lydney

---

An easy walk through wildlife-rich woodland to the heart of Dean's ancient iron delvings. One modest climb in woodland.

The Village Inn (0594) 564555

For many years The Rising Sun, owned by Perretts, then West Country Brewery (hence the Castle plaque), The Village Inn enjoys a commanding position at virtually the highest point in the village. In summer, from tables on the patio, may be had one of the most extensive views from any pub in Dean, an unbroken vista stretching across thousands of acres of forest and over scores of slades, villages and lesser viewpoints.

Nearer to hand the village cricket club use that greenest of mowers, sheep, to trim the square (gives a new meaning to the phrase "sticky wicket"...). Beyond the nearby Forest stone War Memorial is a rough lane called Sun Tump; was this named after the pub or did the pub's builders take an ages-old name for their own?

The old Rising Sun has been completely gutted and extended, reopening in Summer 1992; it's difficult now to appreciate that this building is one of the oldest in Bream, first licensed well over 300 years ago. The bar, offering Marston's Pedigree, is surprisingly small, opening on to a comfy drinking area dotted with stools and benches and decorated largely with mirrors and dried flowers; there's a separate eating area up a few steps, a much larger restaurant is in the offing.

Opening hours are 11 a.m. – 2.30 p.m. (not Mondays) and 6 p.m. – 11 p.m., standard Sunday hours. A good range of bar meals are available at both sessions.

The Walk

Turn left from the Inn, crest the hill and walk down the High Street to the main road. Towards the end you'll pass the Old Hall on your left, an ancient structure with fine, mullioned windows now surprisingly lying unused and abandoned. Opposite is that ever-lamentable sight, an old pub abandoned to the private housing market.

The Old Hall, Bream.

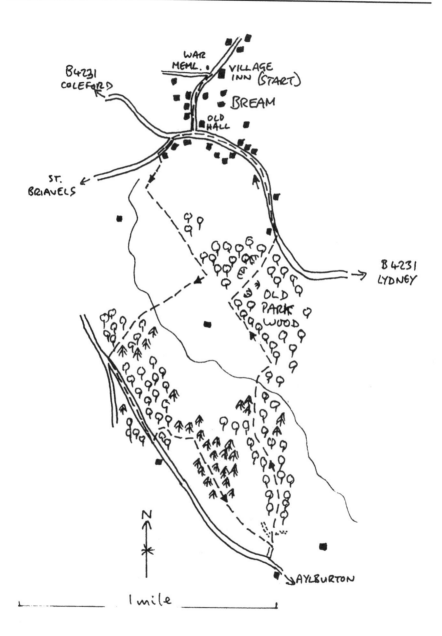

Turn right along the main road, walk down to the corner and fork left towards St. Briavels along Parrawell Road. Immediately past the last house on your left – a hundred yards or so – climb the stile beside the metal field gate and bear slightly right, heading for the gap in the double line of fence that runs the breadth of the field. Once through this turn right and walk to the stile in the hedgerow ahead.

Your route is left along the track. In the field on your right stands a memorial hidden beneath a holly tree and beside a spring; it's dedicated to "I Frederick Gosling, Vicar of Bream 1869-82", probably a very popular parson, a proponent of clean water supplies...or both?

Walk a few yards up the track to the corner and climb the gate beside the broken down stile, then keep the hedge to your left and walk up the gentle incline of Broom Hill. Splendid views develop down the wooded valley of Park Brook and across the Severn Estuary to the green heights beyond.

At the end of this long field climb the two stiles and turn right, then follow the path around the crest of Broom Hill and over a further stile to end up at a corner of woodland. Climb the well hidden stile here and work steeply downhill to the footbridge across the stream in this wooded valley. Beyond this start the moderate ascent up through these mixed woodlands, keeping fairly close to the wall on your left. Go straight over the track you reach then let the wall fade away slightly to the left, in a short distance you'll emerge onto a minor road at a junction. Turn sharp left towards Aylburton and Lydney.

Stick with this quiet backroad for about half a mile, the woods on either side a mix of deciduous and coniferous species bordered, on your right, by a deep growth of rhododendrons offering a blaze of colour in the spring. The copious wildflowers attract a large number of majestic butterflies, in particular the spectacular peacock.

Not far after the woods on your right peter out, a public footpath sign points the way, left, along a forestry road. Wind round with this, bordering the top edge of an impenetrable conifer plantation, and continue along the grassy track to the far end of the stand of massive firs on your left. Here there are three choices of path, choose the waymarked middle one (slightly to your left) which burrows into the spruces; remarkably, the forestry road to the left has a "no entry" symbol!

The path snakes through this rather gloomy woodland, spangles of light here and there cascading through to the forest floor. This type of woodland is a favourite haunt of the Goldcrest (England's second smallest bird), Crossbill and coal tit. You'll probably also hear the mewing call of a buzzard circling overhead or perched atop one of the taller trees.

Follow the occasional waymark through the wood and climb the stile at the far end, then following the wide path gradually downhill through the fairly recently harvested and replanted area. There are excellent views across the Severn to Sharpness Docks and Berkeley Power Station (if there is such a thing as an excellent view of a power station...), Lydney Docks on the near bank and, off to your right, the graceful sweep of the great bridge across the estuary.

The valley into which you're gradually falling is largely a part of the Estate of Lydney Park, the large Victorian mansion home of Viscount Bledisloe. Generations of this family have developed a renowned woodland garden of azaleas, rhododendrons, more exotic species and a wide variety of rare trees and shrubs. The Estate also contains one of the best preserved Roman Temples – this one to the pagan Celtic god Nodens – in Britain.

Climb the stile beside the gate at the bottom and follow the path/track for a further fifty or so yards to the next metal gate. Don't go through this, rather turn left and walk alongside the wall for a short distance before this forestry road enters the lovely woodland of Lower Bargains Wood. Carry on into the trees, take the first right fork (ignore the old, indistinct fork just as you enter the trees) then, a short distance later, take the left fork onto a slightly greener roadway. This is your route for nearly a mile, falling gently through majestic stands of oak and beech towards Park Brook. You may be lucky to see a Roe Deer or two here whilst squirrels and birdlife abound in this peaceful, out-of-the-way corner of Dean.

Persevere through areas of high bracken which bracket the track and, at the far end of a stand of very tall firs, fork right to the Brook and ford it on the rough stepping stones. Climb up the trackway beyond to the small clearing at the top. Here turn left and climb the stile at the top corner of the meadow, then follow this thistlebound top edge across two meadows. About fifty yards into the third meadow climb the stile on the right and enter the woods to be faced immediately by the empty sockets of two old limekilns. Pass to the right of these and dodge through the trees with the path to reach a wide forestry road, turning right along this.

This is Upper Old Park Wood, the principal area of the roman and medieval ironworking – scowles – remains in Dean. These ancient woodlands are pitted with gorges, labyrinths and hollows, isolated pillars and stumps of limestone and jumbled areas of fallen boulders.

The rich, lush undergrowth of ivies, ferns and creepers, great old beech, ash and oaks and gnarled old holly and yew trees which seem to grow from the very rock produce a modest sized area of secret landscape, generally known as the Devil's Chapel. Much of it is visible from the forestry road which dips and weaves through the area and is the only public right of way through these private woods; the evidence is that many people venture off into the winding chasms, which can prove dangerous as the undergrowth often hides steep pits and hollows. Some extraction of ore continued, spasmodically, in Lydney Park until late last century, the ore being transferred to a railhead near Whitecroft via a trolley road.

The forestry road eventually issues onto the main Bream to Lydney road. Turn left and walk the remaining half mile back to Bream, turning right up High Street to return to the Inn.

22. Bicslade

Route: Parkend – Cannop Ponds – Bixhead – Bix Slade – Nagshead

Distance: 6.5 miles

Map: O.S. Outdoor Leisure Sheet 14, Wye Valley & Forest of Dean

Start: The Fountain Inn, Parkend village centre. G.R. 616078

Access: Parkend is about four miles southeast of Coleford and five miles north of Lydney, well signposted from both towns. The Fountain is near the old railway station.

Bus: Regular service W25 from Lydney (Mondays-Fridays and two Saturday buses).

A fascinating glimpse at many of the industries Dean has nurtured over the centuries. An easy walk based largely on forestry roads and passing through a leading nature reserve.

The Fountain Inn (0594 562189)

Just off the village green and a stones throw from the old station, this is one of two surviving pubs in the village; there were once many others, largely beerhouses used almost solely by, for example, workers in the furnaces or collieries to which these beerhouses were attached.

A recent transformation has seen The Fountain changed from a rather dowdy, musty old retreat to a pleasant, airy concern renowned for its food and offering Bass, Worthington and at least one guest beer, often from a small or distant brewery (e.g. Butcombe, or Mitchell's from Lancaster). The Inn itself is about two centuries old, originating as a beerhouse and growing considerably in size when the railway arrived.

The walls and beams, shelves and alcoves are hung with an incredibly varied collection of artefacts, many of which reflect the old industries on which Parkend was founded. For the musically inclined there's a piano ... and a washboard. What space isn't taken by oddities is filled by potted plants, old photos of the local area, or the pub cats. Behind the pub is a small beer garden, beside a stream shaded by massive beech and lime trees.

Opening hours are 11.30 a.m. – 3 p.m. and 6 p.m. – 11 p.m., all day (11.30 a.m. – 11 p.m.) Saturdays, standard Sunday hours. The considerable menu choice includes a good range of curries. Children are welcome, and this is one of the few Forest pubs which offers accommodation.

Parkend

Parkend once hummed with activity. Furnaces and forges, collieries, tinplate works, the railway and stoneworks employed many hundreds of people until the end of the last century. The collieries, Parkend Main and Parkend Royal for example, were some of the most productive in the Forest, annually producing considerably over 100,000 tons a year. Their remains, gradually being cloaked over by undergrowth or deliberate planting, are still visible to the east of the village. The tallest building in Parkend, the imposing field studies centre, is all that remains of Parkend Ironworks. It was once the engine house, housing the steam engine which provided the blast for the furnaces, a blast originally worked by a massive waterwheel, 51 feet in diameter. Just north of here the rough pastures mark the site of the tinplate works.

The old railway station, immediately south of the engine house, is virtually the only other survivor of Parkend's heyday, and itself barely clings to life. The line between Lydney and Parkend was used by B.R. until the late 1970s to convey roadstone from sidings opposite The Fountain Inn. As this trade gradually faded the line was offered to the Dean Forest Railway who used Parkend Station as their base. More recently their collection of steam locomotives and rolling stock has been transferred to Norchard, near Lydney, leaving Parkend Station to decay as a rusting siding, the weeds only occasionally disturbed as an odd wagon or carriage is moved for storage.

Today's industry is based on the most obvious of the Forest's products, wood, with a sawmills and plywood manufacture providing much needed local work. The old railway and tramroad tracks are largely pleasant walkways – this walk follows the route of some of these –

radiating from the village which, more or less, slumbers within the encroaching forest. Around the vast village green is a hotch-potch of cottages, chapels, old shops and grander houses which tend to typify a redundant industrial settlement, be it in Gloucestershire or Lancashire, Northumberland or Cornwall. Few, however, could claim the verdant setting of Parkend.

The Walk

Turn right from the pub to reach the crossroads beside the old station, its forlorn shelters, footbridge and rusting rails an echo of busier times. Here turn left, walking past the old engine house, now resplendent in a mantle of Virginia Creeper, and the site of the old tinplate works.

At the T-junction turn right and walk away from the village green. The building immediately before the old level crossing is one of the village's lost pubs, formerly the Railway Inn which closed in 1959.

Once over the crossing, turn left along the road signposted for Lydbrook and walk along to the beginning of the woods on your right. Here, a Forestry Commission signboard announces the location as the Cannop Valley. Turn right here along the forestry road, virtually opposite the entrance to the Remploy factory, and follow it into the mature mixed oak and beech woodland.

Shortly before reaching a junction of roadways you'll cross an old, overgrown leat. This is Ironworks Leat, the power stream for the massive waterwheel at Parkend Furnace, snaking down from the ponds higher up the valley. At the junction bear left and follow the narrower roadway alongside the fir plantation, with the mature broadleaf woods gradually thickening on your left. Some of these forestry roads, common throughout the whole of Dean, have a surprising raison d'etre. Useful as they are to the Forestry Commission as a management tool, many were constructed by the U.S. Army during the Second War to facilitate the movement of ammunition to and beneath the trees; secure from aerial observation, the Forest's canopy offered protection for major dumps of bombs and other munitions.

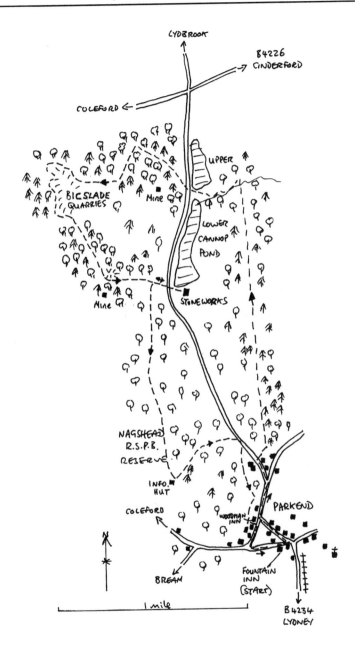

Forest Track, near Parkend

At one point in the trees to your left are the scant remains of an old adit, or coal scraping. Climb the stile at the cross-tracks and continue ahead, the broadleaf trees giving way, for a short while at least, to characterless, serried ranks of firs.

Once across a small brook, climb the waymarked stile on the left and wind with the path down the course of this brook. Here and there narrow seams of shaley coal are exposed in the steep, broken banks of this watercourse. Beyond the old railway line at the end of the path is Upper Cannop Pond. Nowadays, a valuable wildfowl refuge and popular picnicking spot, this, and the nearby Lower Pond were created in the 1820s as reservoirs to serve furnaces at Parkend, the water powering the massive 51' diameter waterwheel, claimed as the second largest in the Kingdom, to work the furnace blast.

Cross the bridge and the dam, then go straight over the main road and up the rutted forestry road immediately to the left of the car park. Here the walk joins with several of the family of colour-waymarked paths developed by the Forestry Commission in recent years. Go left at the red/green waymarked post and climb gently through the firs to another forestry road. Go straight over this with the red waymark, continuing to climb out of the valley. At the fork of paths by the creeper-clad tree bear left, then follow the red waymarkers up to a further forestry road.

Pausing for breath here, it's worth diverting left along this roadway for a short distance where, a little way uphill, there are glimpses from the side-road to your left of a freeminers gale, this one a well established feature of many years standing. Retrace your steps to the point you met the roadway and look carefully at the adjoining tree. The tattered, scraped bark is evidence of deer rubbing their antlers against the tree, possibly to rid the antlers of the velvety covering which antlers sport for part of the year.

Re-enter the trees opposite this point and continue uphill. Turn left up the next forestry road and walk to and through the clearing near the top. Views from here, Barnhills Plantation, show both how far you've climbed and the great extent of Dean's woodlands; there's hardly a tree-free yard to be seen. Bear right with the track at the top end of the clearing to reach a crossing of tracks. Go straight over, soon to emerge from the trees at the lip of Bicslade Quarries. Bear right and follow the rough road around the lip of the quarries.

These present a rather unexpected, eerie landscape, the great abysses, chambers and jumbled piles of waste dotted by rusting old cranes, their great black supporting legs and beams like gigantic spiders waiting to pounce. The place just aches to be used as the set for Doctor Who. It's a particularly other-worldly place in the depths of winter, the quarry-bottom pools frozen over, great sheets of ice defying gravity by developing on the exposed root systems of trees which break through the sheer cliff faces and massive icicles drooping from overhangs. Disused for several years, one quarry is now producing stone again. Keeping a close eye on the great slabs and spoil heaps will be repaid by finding fragments of fossilised trees, corals and shells.

The undressed stone is today carried to stoneworks by lorry. Until 1946, a horse drawn tramway served this function. The route of it, down lonely Bix Slade, is still marked by the stone-block sleepers to which iron rails were once bolted. To find this turn left along the line of the electricity cables at the far end of the workings, near to a long old corrugated iron hut. Bear first left, pass the old crane off to your left and follow this developing track half left, down into the valley of Bicslade (or Bixslade).

This is a glorious section of the walk, tumbled, moss and lichen covered blocks of stone protruding from the thick, mixed birch, oak and fir woods which clothe the steep sides of the winding valley (slade is a Forest term for valley). On either side of the tramroad at one point are remains of two old gales, certainly working in the late 1970s but now gradually being reclaimed by the forest; in the same general area is a fenced-off old shaft.

About half way down the tramroad bends left, a point marked on its left by a small quarry which, again, has recently seen extraction after years of dereliction. This used to be an excellent spot for finding the fossilised traces of feather-like ferns in the massive slabs of rock beside the track; perhaps the new workings will expose replacements.

Continue down the tramroad, following the lines of sleeper-blocks. Off to the right, a few yards up along the dark, muddy roadway is another of this area's gales, a smaller concern than the one chanced upon earlier and easily viewed from the wooded track.

Return to the tramroad and follow its line to the road at the bottom. Cross straight over this and walk the few yards to the stoneworks. This is in many ways a fascinating survival, an echo of the Forest of many decades ago. You can see all the processes from outside the perimeter fence, the conversion of the basic Forest stone to dressed blocks highly prized for its colour and durability. Note, too, a remaining section of tramroad rail – or plate – protruding through the rough surface of the lay-by. The rails once ran across the dam which holds back Lower Cannop Pond, above the stoneworks, and on to an interchange wharf with the Severn and Wye Railway whence massive blocks of Forest Bluestone were exported throughout the country.

Stoneworks, Cannop Ponds

Recross the road and retrace your steps back up the tramroad for about 150 yards to the green/yellow waymarker on your left. Go left here and follow the obvious path into the woods, crossing several stiles. This magnificent area of mature oak and beech woodland is Nagshead Plantation; many of the trees are over 200 years old and constitute one of the best tracts of broadleaf woodland in Dean.

Much of it is managed as a Nature Reserve by the R.S.P.B., which organisation maintains a small information centre in the Plantation. To reach this continue along the wide path and bear left at the fork by the bench.

Follow the yellow arrows, climb the wide stile and walk through the bower of holly trees, then go through the unusual metal stile to reach the hut. It's open infrequently, but the nearby information board is regularly updated with news of the latest bird sightings and locations.

Parkend is now not far away. Facing the hut, turn left and follow the green waymarked route down through the open pasture and the gap in the massive cupressor hedge/windbreak. At the bottom of the woods beyond turn right along the old railway line and remain with this, bearing half-right at the end and walk behind Hughes Terrace.

About half way along, a narrow pathway leads down left beside The Woodman pub (look for the garden tables), the other surviving village pub, this one offering Marston's Pedigree and Flowers on draught. Opposite is the immense village green, skirt this round to the right to return to The Fountain.

23. Gatcombe

Route: Purton – Etloe – Gatcombe

Distance: 3 miles

Map: O.S. Outdoor Leisure Sheet 14, Wye Valley & Forest of Dean

Start: Purton. G.R. SO 671046

Access: The hamlet of Purton is about a mile and a half east of the A48, some three miles north of Lydney. Look for roadsigns for Purton (and also the brown "bed symbol" tourist signs) off the A48 and follow the very narrow roads to the Hotel.

An easy walk near to and alongside the Severn Estuary visiting a hidden, long disused old port. Some sections may be muddy after high tide.

The Old Severn Bridge Hotel (0594 842454)

Lovers of out-of-the-way old pubs will find this one a treat. It was originally built in the early 1600s, virtually next door to the old Purton Manor House, home (for a while at least) of that renowned explorer and adventurer Sir Walter Raleigh. It's not redolent of those days of yore, however, being more of a mix of cosy little inglenook rooms and large, period style drawing rooms. The bar is in one of these latter, the huge windows of which allow sweeping views across the great expanse of the Severn Estuary.

The pub stands atop one of the many ridges of sandstone which have created a series of river-cliffs along the Estuary. Between the pub and the water, carried on an embankment above the river, the main Gloucester to South Wales railway runs above the tidal creeks and mudflats. It's invisible from the pub, and the large beer garden which takes full advantage of this prime position, but you certainly know it's there when a train grumbles past, occasionally a steam engine as this is one of the routes over which British Rail allows steam specials to operate.

Other old vehicles appear at the Hotel on the third Tuesday evening of each month when the local old car club meets there.

The Old Severn Bridge, after which the hotel is named, was a substantial iron railway bridge across the Severn a few hundred yards to the south. A rudderless, uncontrollable oil barge was swept into it one night in 1960, felling some of the spans. It was never repaired, much of the rail network it once supported was closed in the early 1960s and the remaining bridge spans demolished and blown up in 1967.

There are several old photographs of this structure in the main bar, together with an indenture recording property transactions carried out when the railway was first built, by The South Wales Railway in 1851.

Opening hours are 12 noon – 3 p.m. (not Mondays) and 7 p.m. – 11 p.m., when the beers which can be sampled may be Smiles, Hook Norton, Pedigree or a variety of others, depending on the whim of the owner. There's also a substantial bar meals menu to choose from.

The Walk

Join the narrow road which snakes down in front of the Hotel (easily accessed down the steps from the beer garden) and follow it over Lanes Brook and up through the band of woodland beyond. The brook flows beneath the railway bridge into Purton Pill, an insignificant gap in the great Severnside mudbanks which, nonetheless, once supported a small boatbuilding yard.

The arched bridge which marks the end of the woods is virtually all that remains of the ill-fated Purton Steam Carriage Road, an early attempt to link the Forest's coal and ironfields with the Severn, where a port was planned for Purton. These arches date from around 1832, initial work on the planned dock was obliterated by the main line some years later. The scheme ran into both financial difficulties and strong opposition, and was superseded by other more successful projects, such as the lines to Bullo Pill and Lydney Harbour.

Remain with this quiet backroad for a little over a mile, passing through the pleasant hamlet of Etloe, no more than a string of old cottages and

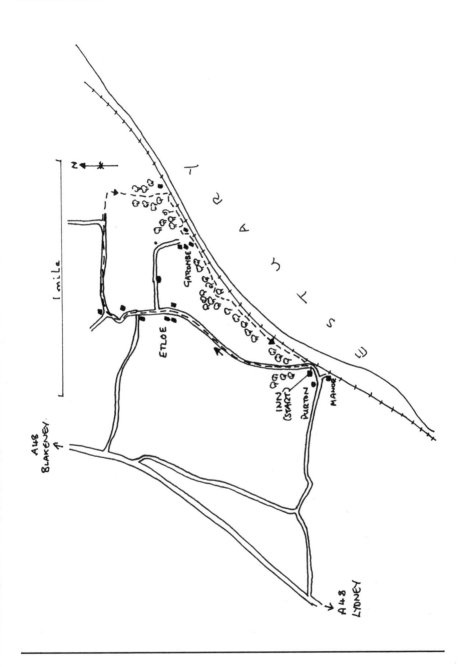

farms, including the fine Georgian court dated 1730. At the triàngular junction keep right, towards Awre and Blakeney, and at the next junction steer right again, heading for Awre. The tall hedgerows along this stretch of back lane are heavily laden with wild hops, very distinctive during September.

Progressing along the lane, the hedges become much lower allowing extensive views, left, up the Vale of Severn and to your right across the Severn to the Cotswolds. In about half a mile, as the road bends left, go straight ahead along the "No Through Road." A further 250 yards brings you to two field gates on your right, go through the first of these (the rusty metal one) and follow the old cartway beyond to the sheep pens at the far end. Go ahead through the gate here and wind down this rough lane into the woods.

At the bottom end, as this track swings left to the isolated cottage, continue straight ahead across the pasture to the stile at the far side, at the foot of the railway embankment. Climb this and turn immediately right, shortly reaching another one in front of two old lime kilns. A steep set of steps built into the hillside leads up to the crest of one of many river cliffs in the area. Gaps in the trees allow views across the Estuary to the Cotswolds, whilst on the far shore of the river you can pick out a number of old barges, long past their use-by date, slowly rotting away.

The path continues along the lip of the cliff, bounded by mature oak/beech woods. Climb the stile at the end and turn right, following the path round a further bend and down a long, gradual series of steps to a surfaced lane. Turn left here into Gatcombe hamlet.

This idyllic spot was once a busy little port (witness the Old Customs House) and boatbuilding centre, in 1834 for example a Snow (type of boat), "Thomas", weighing in at 129 tons was launched here. This was late in the day, however, several centuries before naval craft were assembled here and Sir Francis Drake lived at the imposing pink-painted house near the foreshore. Nothing now remains of this old industry or the port.

Beside the row of cottages, a few old boats are slowly rotting, opposite them the pile of funnel-shaped wire baskets are salmon putches, placed in the inter-tidal zone beyond the railway arches on frameworks which hold them in mid-water, hopefully capturing a valuable fish or three. The old rotting boats are "Stopper Boats," used in an alternative way of salmon fishing, a rather involved method based on wires attached to both shore and a weighty anchor and deep nets slung between wooden poles; the practice is now all but extinct.

The little port lost its livelihood both to the railway and to the Gloucester and Sharpness Canal, the seaward end of which is marked by the tall silos on the far bank of the Estuary (there's a footpath locals use which crosses the railway line near Drake's House, from which you can see this complex and, downstream on this bank, the white-painted Purton Manor). Before these blows, much trade in spices, alcohol and other 'excisable' goods was transhipped here by merchants based in Gloucester (hence the Old Customs House).

Purton Old Manor and the Severn Estuary

Leave Gatcombe along the track which runs between the cottages and the railway arches and follow the woodside path beyond over the stile and into the small pasture. Stick to the right hand side of this, cross the next stile and climb the set of steps up through the band of woodland.

At the top end of the trees turn left along the edge of the field and walk around to the path which forks left, down into a further wooded dingle. Steep steps lead down to a solid footbridge, beyond which a steep scramble and further steps end at a stile.

Beyond this, keep the trees on your left and walk along the top of this wooded river cliff. At one point is an old boundary post dated 1882, marking the edge of the Great Western Railway's property along the Estuary's foreshore.

At the end of the pastures descend the further long flight of steps down into the trees, ending up at a stone-slab footbridge over Lanes Brook. Beyond this, walk up to the road and bear left to complete the final few yards to The Old Hotel.

24. Lancaut

Route: Chepstow – Offa's Dyke – Lancaut – Wintour's Leap

Distance: 5 miles

Map: O.S. Outdoor Leisure Sheet 14, Wye Valley & Forest of Dean

Start: Chepstow Town Centre, by the Old Wye Bridge

Access: Ample free parking in Chepstow; the Bridge Inn is at the Welsh end of the old bridge at the junction of Bridge Street with The Back.

An easy walk down into the most spectacular section of the Wye Gorge, passing through a nature reserve to an abandoned old church.

The Bridge Inn (0291 625622)

A small convivial local at the site of Chepstow's old port, this picturesque old inn dates back to the Seventeenth Century, originating as the "Ship and Castle" Inn. A short history of the pub and its licensees is given on a board mounted above the fireplace in the flag-floored back area of the one large room, the best place for muddy boots to find a welcome.

The wood-panelled bar dominates the public areas, largely carpeted and comfortably furnished, the walls hung with nondescript prints, beams, alcoves and shelves sporting a fair collection of old bottles and flagons. The flagged area hosts the most interesting decoration, old photographs and maps of the once-thriving river port and the shipyards which flourished well into this century.

The Bridge is a free house, but most of the beers seem to come from the Welsh Brewers (Bass) stable – Hancocks HB, Worthington Best and Bass, but there are two spare handpumps offering a wide variety of guest ales, Fullers on my last visit for example. The pub is open all day (standard Sunday hours) and bar meals are available virtually throughout.

The Walk

Head across Rennie's majestic cast-iron bridge, dating from 1816 and one of the earliest such constructions. Half way across, the boundary between Monmouthshire and Gloucestershire, the Welsh/English border, is celebrated in cast iron.

The contrast between the Wye at low and high tide levels here is marked. At its lowest, it seems little more than a stream coursing between massive shoulders of mud, dotted with small boats and yachts dipping at alarming angles; these great, glistening cliffs of mud dramatically enhance the already commanding presence of the castle, a few yards upstream. At high tide it can be like a millpond, the Severn estuary, just a mile or so downstream, effectively stemming the flow of the Wye leaving it still and serene, gently lapping the edges of the old quays and the foot of the great limestone cliffs.

At the far end of the bridge go virtually straight ahead, past the metal barriers and up the walled, tarmaced path which climbs steeply up the hillside. Ignore the path off to the right about half way up (which is the very last [or first...] mile or so of Offa's Dyke Path) and continue up to the main road.

Cross straight over this and go up the lane opposite, Mopla Road. As this bends round to the right climb the stile on your left and walk up the field path alongside the house. This is a well-trodden route, part of Offa's Dyke Path which you walk for the next half mile or so. Behind the bungalow at the crest of the hill is a ruined round tower, marked on maps as a lookout tower, logic suggests it is associated with the castle, a fine view over which is to be had from here.

Simply follow the frequent waymark arrows/acorns through the pastures and alongside the estate wall of the house to your left, soon ending up walking across a field heading for the left of the substantial mansion of Pen Moel, built early this century for Lord Waring. Climb the stile by the little wooden overbridge here and pass beneath this, leaving Offa's Dyke Path, at least for the time-being. The path starts its sometimes steep descent down these steep, wooded slopes of the Wye Gorge, all now a part of Lancaut Nature Reserve, managed by the Gloucestershire Trust for Nature Conservation.

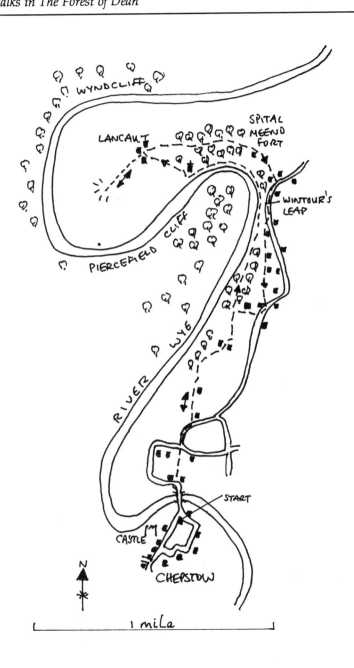

The woodlands are a fine mix of gnarled old yews, birches, oaks and massive beeches, undergrown by a sometimes thick forest of buddleia. On your right, the great limestone cliffs tower above, the haunt of jackdaws and seagulls. To your left gaps in the trees reveal inspiring views across the river to the great cliffs at Wyndcliff. At one point the woods have been swept away by a substantial rockfall, probably the result of quarrying which took place until fairly recently at the lip of the gorge above.

Pick your way across this and continue along the obvious path back into the trees beyond. The path rises and falls through the woods, never reaching the muddy riverbank. At one point it joins a major cross-path beneath a massive cliff, bear left here and then keep left at the various forks to, eventually, fall to the level of the riverbank here on Lancaut Peninsular. The name Lancaut is held to derive from "The Church of St. Cewydd," a Welsh Saint of the Dark Ages.

Stay with the path just inside the trees where possible as the riverside path is very muddy (and may be covered at the highest flood tides). At one point the woods peel back beneath the site of an old quarry. Keep left here, following the direction indicated by the yellow arrow painted on the isolated boulder. From here are stunning views both upstream and downstream, the great tracts of hanging woodlands particularly attractive in their vivid autumnal hues.

Climb the metal stile and walk on for about thirty yards, then turn right with the waymark painted on the post and walk up to the ruins. This was St. James's Church, originally built in about 1190 as a Chapel of Ease but elevated to full Parish Church status a century or so later. Presumably it was built on the site first selected for St. Cewydd's church, of which nothing is known.

As with a lot of isolated rural churches, it's difficult to see from where it would have drawn its parishioners, but despite this it survived in regular use until the 1860s. Its great treasure was an early medieval lead font, one of only 38 known; when the church was abandoned Gloucester Cathedral quickly laid claim to this particular item. The roofless ruins retain vestiges of plaster, a few glassless windows and a weathered stoup in the south wall. What appears to be the only tombstone on the site lies flat in the nave.

Outside the fencing at the top-left corner of the "churchyard" bear half-left up the obvious path through the failing woodland to the pasture beyond. From here, sight the red-tile roofed barn to the right of the house peering over the ridgetop and walk towards this, passing to the left of the great oak and leaving the pasture via the gate opposite the enormous dead treestump, all that remains of a once famous old oak.

Your way lies right, along the driveway, but there is a right of way through the back of the farmyard at Lancaut Farm which leads to an old field road offering glorious views across the great meander of the Wye to the towering cliffs and hanging woodlands at Piercefield and Wyndcliff.

Walk along the driveway and across the cattle-grid. Immediately after this bear right along the narrow path into the woods and follow this, bearing left at the fork in about two hundred yards. This old sunken trackway climbs steadily, shortly passing by the remains of a pair of limekilns, presumably fed from the small, overgrown quarry behind.

The track emerges from the woods onto a minor road, bear right along this and follow it to its end. As this passes the 1950s house it cuts through the ramparts of an old British Hill Fort known as Spital Meend, the band of large oaks, beech and firs mark the line of these ramparts across the neck of the peninsular. Beyond here, as the road bends to the left, views open out across the Severn Estuary to the Cotswolds and Oldbury Nuclear Power Station.

On reaching the main road turn right and walk around the bend, one hundred yards or so past which go right, along the footpath signposted for Sedbury Cliff. Within yards make a detour a few paces to your right, but with a care as the edge of these 300 foot cliffs are unfenced. Views from here are as spectacular as any riverscapes you're likely to find in Britain.

To your left the Wye cuts canal-like through the last section of its famous gorge, ahead and below are the green pastures of the Lancaut Peninsular on which you've walked, whilst in the distance are the highest cliffs on the Wye, Wyndcliff, which in two steps reach to over 750 feet.

The point where you're standing is Wintour's Leap. The story goes that in 1645, during the Civil War, Colonel Winter, a member of a well known and staunchly Royalist local family, was defeated in a skirmish with the Roundheads near Lydney. Pursued by his protagonist, one Colonel Massey, Winter and his horse, to evade capture, rode off the edge of this cliff and plummeted to the mudbanks far below. Sadly the truth is less dramatic, Winter and his brother managing to reach the riverbank near Lancaut and escape by boat to live to fight another day.

Unless you're inclined to emulate this equestrian feat simply follow the path behind the houses and along the edge of the cliffs. At one point, the remains of an old quarry have gnawed away at the edge, the cause of the rockfall passed earlier in the walk.

Walk along the short stretch of driveway in front of the bungalow, from which are glimpses of the Severn Bridge, and continue ahead at the bend along the path beneath a bower of hazel and holly trees.

The steepening path passes through a couple of new kissing gates and soon emerges on the main road. Turn right along this and walk for under one hundred yards to the bottom entrance to Pen Moel, immediately beyond which is, on your right, a kissing gate giving access to the path alongside the estate wall. Pass beneath the small stone bridge and walk to the stile at the far end, on your left just before the wooden bridge. Climb this stile and reverse the initial mile or so of the walk to return to Chepstow.

25. Clanna Woods

Route: Woolaston Common – Clanna Pond – Rodmore – Hewelsfield

Distance: 5 miles

Map: O.S. Outdoor Leisure Sheet 14, Wye Valley & Forest of Dean

Start: The Rising Sun, Woolaston Common, G.R. 590009

Access: Turn off the A48 at the sign for Netherend, about 3 miles SW of Lydney and follow the signs for Hewelsfield. The Rising Sun is on the left in about one mile.

A combination of quiet, little visited woodland, industrial heritage, the Forest's oldest church and great views down the Severn Estuary on this easy walk which will be muddy after rain.

The Rising Sun (0594 529282)

The first record of a pub here is in 1876 when the Rising Sun is listed as a beerhouse, one of a handful serving the developing community of Woolaston Common. These folk were mostly miners from Dean, staking a claim to patches of the extensive common land and constructing basic cottages or hovels, the basis of many of today's "desirable country cottages" which dot the landscape here.

The Rising Sun originated as a barn and two cottages, made obvious by the rather peculiar shape of today's building. Within is a large, comfortable lounge area, sparsely decorated with frames full of banknote collections and unusually free of the brasses and plates associated with country pubs. The windows look out over pastures to a beautiful little wooded valley, a view also enjoyable from a few tables on the patio. Above and around the bar area is a huge collection of (empty) whisky bottles, the real McCoy, not the more commonly found miniatures.

Beers on offer on a regular basis are Theakston's Best Bitter, Hook Norton Best Bitter and Thwaites (from Blackburn), in summer there's an additional one or more also available. Opening hours are 12 noon – 2.30 p.m. (not Wednesdays) and 6.30 p.m. – 11 p.m.; Sunday hours are 12 noon – 2.30 p.m., 7 p.m. – 10.30 p.m.. Bar meals are available until about an hour before closing. If the weather's fit there are a few tables in the garden to the rear, overlooking a shallow valley to the distant wooded hills through which the walk passes. There's also a separate public bar for those with fearsomely muddy boots.

The Walk

On leaving the pub, turn left up the narrow road and continue along it for about half a mile to the junction with Sand Tump lane, on your left. On the right here a narrow path falls away beside the cream-painted garden wall and across the lively brook on a slab footbridge. Once across this turn right, then left and climb uphill alongside the fence. Stay with this line to reach a minor road, cross straight over and walk through the field beyond.

At the far right hand corner climb the stile and work down to the Cone Brook, cross the slab bridge and scramble straight up the steep pasture to the stile at the top. From here walk up the rough road which, within yards, bends to the right. In a short distance on the right is the entrance to a farm, opposite this a forestry road leads into Clanna Woods.

Walk down this for a few yards, then bear right along the path through the trees, almost immediately picking up the course of a well overgrown mill leat on your right. Remain with this for several hundred yards until the point where the leat widens out, marking the site of the old pond which fed the leat; some of the old dam wall is still there, smothered by the undergrowth.

Here, turn left down the short, steep, narrow path, cross straight over the wider track at the bottom and continue down the path through the trees beyond. Cross the wooden footbridge, then turn right over the slab bridge and climb the wooden stepped path. Just a few yards beyond the end of these steps branch off this main path to the right, at the point where an old tree stump remains in the line of the path. An, at first,

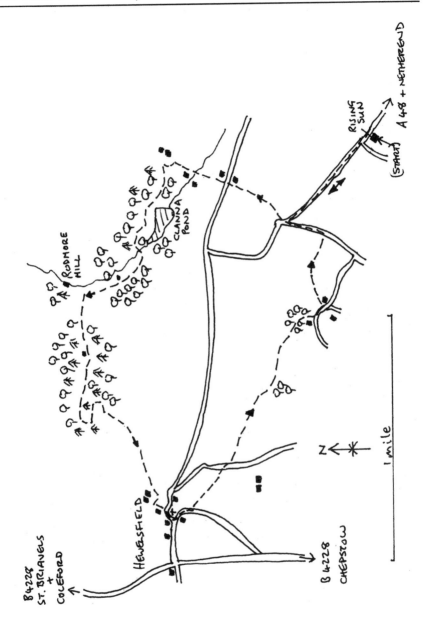

Clanna Woods

indistinct path meanders through the spurge laurel undergrowth of these fir woods. It gradually becomes more obvious towards the far end of the pond, off to your left beyond the trees.

The pond is Clanna Pond, initially created in the late 1600s to power the bellows and hammers of an iron forge which existed a short distance below the pond. This is later recorded as being converted into a paper/cardboard mill, surviving as such until at least the end of the last century. The tiny Cone Brook supplies the pond's water. This isolated valley once hummed with industrial activity, with forges, an iron furnace at Rodmore, several paper mills, corn mills and saw mills. All are now gone, though some buildings remain, either in ruins or converted to private houses whilst Clanna Woods hide a wealth of mill leats, ponds and marshy pools.

At the far end of the woods the path emerges onto a forestry road beside a bridge over a waterfall, the downfall between an overgrown upper pond and Clanna Pond. Cross this bridge and walk to the surfaced road, then turn right along this.

In about half a mile, the rebuilt Rodmore Mill comes into view. Just as the road bends right to approach this building go left through the double gate (there's a waymark arrow here) and walk up along the rough road, woodland on your right. A powerful stream has cut a miniature gorge hereabouts. In dry weather, this stream emerges from strong springs in the valleyside just beyond the gate across the roadway, higher upstream the riverbed is all but dry, trickles issuing here and there at the junction between the limestone and sandstone rocks.

Go left at the fork and walk up beside the small pumping station, continuing beyond to the clearing in the woods at the point where the road bends left. From this clearing follow the road round to the left and remain with it as open fields appear on the right. Where the woods start again on your right leave the road and walk up through the undergrowth at the edge of these woods, keeping close to the fence on your right. At the point where this bends sharp left are the remains of an old gateway, the gatepost thrown down and the entrance wired off. This marks the start of the public footpath, a new stile should be installed during the winter of 1992/93.

Once in the field, aim to walk through the area of rotting trees/stumps and down into the shallow valley, roughly along the line of the wooden pylons. Walk up this dry valley for a short distance to the second pylon, at the junction of two hedges. Climb the fence on the right here (or the new stile if provided) immediately above the hedge and walk diagonally up across this massive field.

A group of large barns soon comes into view, aim for the left side of these where a couple of gates give access to the driveway of Hewelsfield Court Farm. Walk along this and bear right, then left to reach the old church at Hewelsfield.

This is the centre of the hamlet, a few old farms, villas and houses whose history goes back to Saxon times. Parts of St. Mary Magdalene's Church go back as far, and there are fine Norman arches helping support the squat little tower which houses a peal of bells, one of which is nearly 550 years old.

St. Mary Magdalene Church, Hewelsfield.

The church is at the hub of an unusual circular churchyard, liberally supplied with venerable old tombstones and more grand memorials, many of which slumber beneath great growths of ivy, although the glory of the yard is the massive ancient yew tree, probably as old as the church itself.

Leave the hamlet by the narrow lane to the right of the church lychgate (as seen from outside the churchyard) and wind along this to a point just beyond the last house on your left. Here, a rough track leads left to a field gate, beside which is a stile. Climb this and head across the huge field, aiming to pass just to the right of the isolated oak. Aim then roughly for the middle of the hedge at the far side, looking for the stile marked by a tall post. Once over this, and the one beyond the minor road, walk up along the line of hedge.

As you crest the ridge here a grand panorama unfolds. The horizon ahead is the Cotswold Hills; much of their length is visible from this modest viewpoint. In the foreground the upper Severn Estuary, at low water a great expanse of mud and sandbanks dotted with isolated pools and cut by short, deep creeks.

Two structures which stand out on the far bank are the squat reactor buildings at Berkeley nuclear power station and the tall silos at Sharpness Docks, the thriving little port at this "seaward" end of the Gloucester and Sharpness Canal. Most ships now are unloaded here rather than continuing up the canal to the old wharves at the heart of the medieval City. Off to your right and far to the south, the smudge on the horizon are the Mendip Hills in Somerset.

Swap sides of the hedge at the next stile and continue gradually downhill. At the next stile the direction suggested by the waymark arrow is deceptive, you need to head for the field corner virtually straight ahead of you, just beyond the isolated stand of trees and identified by a couple of rusty corrugated iron sheets.

Climb the rickety stile here and follow the fence to the corner of the woodland. Enter this via a further stile and descend the narrow path through the trees, emerging at the corner of a large garden. Keep left to find a stile, once over which turn right along the old cart track to the minor road.

Walk left along this for a short distance, then go through the black, wooden five-bar-gate just your side of the cream cottage. A series of stiles leads down through the old orchard and rough horse pastures to the end of a rough lane at the edge of the village common – "solely for the use of parishioners" the old notice informs wayfarers.

Walk down the lane, which in a short distance becomes tarmaced, turn left at the T-junction and walk down the minor road. At the bottom turn right to return to the Rising Sun.

The Severn Estuary from Hewelsfield.